JUMPST
THINKING SK
PROBLEM S

Jumpstart! Thinking Skills and Problem Solving presents a collection of simple to use, multi-sensory games and activities which will jumpstart students' understanding of problem solving in action. If you are one of the thousands of teachers looking for a range of practical and fun ideas to engage pupils in effective, proactive learning, then this is the perfect book for you.

Specifically written to help teachers work within the guidelines of the new curriculum, the book will help pupils to explore and learn a wide range of problem-solving and independent thinking skills in an atmosphere of fun, mutual support and tolerance.

Sections within the book reflect key areas of the new curriculum and offer a treasure trove of ideas for building problem-solving and thinking skills into daily teaching. Tried and tested methods of helping children 'learn how to learn' are provided. Areas covered include:

- building problem-solving confidence
- thinking and problem solving in literacy and science
- problem solving in philosophy
- emotional resourcefulness and life skills.

This indispensable, practical book celebrates the joy of critical and independent thinking and will become a vital resource for all classroom teachers at Key Stages 2 and 3.

Steve Bowkett is a former teacher and the author of numerous books for teachers including the bestselling *Jumpstart! Creativity*. He also works as an educational consultant specialising in the areas of thinking skills and problem solving, creativity and literacy.

Jumpstart!

Jumpstart! Thinking Skills and Problem Solving
Games and activities for
ages 7–14
Steve Bowkett

Jumpstart! Maths (2nd Edition)
Maths activities and games for
ages 5–14
John Taylor

Jumpstart! Grammar
Games and activities for
ages 6–14
Pie Corbett and Julia Strong

Jumpstart! Spanish and Italian
Engaging activities for ages 7–12
*Catherine Watts and
Hilary Phillips*

Jumpstart! French and German
Engaging activities for ages 7–12
*Catherine Watts and
Hilary Phillips*

Jumpstart! Drama
Games and activities for
ages 5–11
*Teresa Cremin, Roger McDonald,
Emma Goff and Louise Blakemore*

Jumpstart! Science
Games and activities for
ages 5–11
Rosemary Feasey

Jumpstart! Storymaking
Games and activities for
ages 7–12
Pie Corbett

Jumpstart! Poetry
Games and activities for
ages 7–12
Pie Corbett

Jumpstart! Creativity
Games and activities for
ages 7–14
Steve Bowkett

Jumpstart! ICT
ICT activities and games for
ages 7–14
John Taylor

Jumpstart! Numeracy
Maths activities and games for
ages 5–14
John Taylor

Jumpstart! Literacy
Key Stage 2/3 literacy games
Pie Corbett

JUMPSTART! THINKING SKILLS AND PROBLEM SOLVING

GAMES AND ACTIVITIES FOR AGES 7–14

Steve Bowkett

Routledge
Taylor & Francis Group
LONDON AND NEW YORK

First published 2015
by Routledge
2 Park Square, Milton Park, Abingdon, Oxon OX14 4RN

and by Routledge
711 Third Avenue, New York, NY 10017

Routledge is an imprint of the Taylor & Francis Group, an informa business

British Library Cataloguing in Publication Data
A catalogue record for this book is available from the British Library

Library of Congress Cataloguing in Publication Data
Bowkett, Stephen.
Jumpstart! Thinking skills and problem solving : games and activities for ages 7-14 / Steve Bowkett.
pages cm – (Jumpstart!)
1. Critical thinking–Study and teaching. 2. Problem solving–Study and teaching. 3. Activity programs in education. I. Title.
LB1590.3.B6945 2014
370.15'2–dc23
2014008663

ISBN: 978-1-138-78327-0 (hbk)
ISBN: 978-1-138-78331-7 (pbk)
ISBN: 978-1-315-76873-1 (ebk)

Typeset in Palatino and Scala Sans
by Saxon Graphics Ltd, Derby

MIX
Paper from
responsible sources
FSC
www.fsc.org   FSC® C013056

Printed and bound in Great Britain by
TJ International Ltd, Padstow, Cornwall

Contents

List of figures

Acknowledgements

Grateful thanks to my friend Tony Hitchman for helping me out (again) by creating the artwork for Figures 1.3, 1.7, 1.8, 4.2, 5.2 and 5.3.

Introduction

> We cannot solve our problems with the same level of thinking that created them.
>
> Albert Einstein

Obviously we all think; it is a process that is fundamental to our understanding of the world and our sense of who we are. How we think as much as what we think shapes the judgements we form, the conclusions we reach and the decisions we make. It has been wisely said that while the events of our lives help to mould us as people, it is the choices we make that define us as human beings. Effective and reasoned thinking helps us to make the wisest choices.

As such the purpose of this book is to offer you a collection of insights, ideas, activities and games that will aim to develop your children's ability to think more effectively. The emphasis is on problem solving within the areas of literacy, science, philosophy and emotional resourcefulness, with an initial section dealing with what I've called the 'problem-solving attitude'. My emphasis throughout has been on the processes of thinking that support and guide children's understanding of subject content rather than any substantial reiteration of the content itself. As such in the literacy section, for example, there will be advice and activities on 'editing skills' without explanation of the technicalities of spelling, punctuation and grammar since my presumption has been that such concepts will be covered anyway within the normal syllabus.

A glance through the book will show you that many of the thinking skills required to tackle problems in these areas tend to overlap: certain competencies and dispositions apply generally, not just across the school curriculum but beyond it more broadly in our lives. Thus the activities are designed to complement one another so that developing observation skills in science for instance will prime children to notice the visual difference between your and you're or teacher's and teachers' in literacy (having observed such a distinction children can then be encouraged to wonder what it means). The overall intention therefore is to lay the groundwork to equip children with a 'thinking toolkit' that will be of both immediate and long-lasting benefit.

Developing thinking skills means honing certain potentials the children already possess while introducing them to new strategies for thinking. Ideally this takes place within a classroom environment where children feel happy and confident to contribute their ideas. This is vitally important, since two of the greatest inhibitors to the development of effective thinking are:

- Children's fear of the wrong answer. This is the other side of the 'competitive coin' whereby some children predicate their success on the number of 'right answers' they can summon up from memory on demand combined with making comparative judgements of others. However, simply to know and reiterate facts is not particularly high-level thinking and does not per se demonstrate clear understanding or the ability to think either creatively or critically.
- Teachers doing the children's thinking for them: spoon-feeding ideas so that children become passive and unquestioning recipients of facts rather than active explorers of knowledge.

The clear solution to these problems is for us as educators to let the children do the thinking as far as possible and to value the efforts they make – which brings us back to the whole point of this book.

CREATIVE AND CRITICAL THINKING

Some books on thinking make a distinction between so-called creative thinking and critical thinking skills. My view is that such a separation should be simply a matter of convenience for purposes of explanation. With that in mind, commonly listed critical thinking skills include:

- comparing and contrasting
- sequencing
- predicting
- inferring
- attributing
- prioritising
- determining cause and effect
- deconstructing/analysing.

These kinds of thinking are more deliberate and methodical in their nature; i.e. we need to consciously work our way towards a conclusion.

The so-called creative kinds of thinking operate at a more subconscious level. This means that assimilation and progress towards an outcome take place 'behind the scenes'; our minds are busy even if we aren't aware of it. A common example is when you want to remember a fact – say someone's name – and have that 'on the tip of the tongue' feeling. In those circumstances trying hard to remember generally doesn't work. Usually it's better just to let go of the task but with the clear intention that the name will come to you. Most often it will, and without any effort at all. The thinking that went on to bring that name into consciousness was a subconscious search for that one piece of information (among the countless millions lodged in the memory).

Interestingly, when an answer 'pops out of the blue' like this we often know it is the right name – or that the idea is a good one – partly because we have a *feeling* that is the case and also because usually we can remember all kinds of other things linked to the idea we have just recalled.

The point of mentioning all this is to emphasise the notion that effective thinking is as much a matter of intuition and gut instinct as it is of analysis and reasoning. And this is as pertinent to the sciences as it is to the arts – reading about the history of scientific discoveries and breakthroughs will show that 'moments of illumination' or 'Eureka insights' are common.

Creative kinds of thinking include:

- recognising patterns
- looking at things in different ways (taking a multiple perspective)
- intuiting (noticing your gut feelings and having a sense of what works)
- linking – making fresh connections between previously disparate ideas
- speculating
- visualising (which combines the subconscious free flow of ideas with the conscious construction of mental scenarios).

Practically speaking creative and critical ways of thinking work hand in hand to the benefit of both. When working with children I tell them that the name of the game is 'how many ideas can we have and what use can we make of them?' So at the outset the purpose of our thinking is to generate ideas, options and possibilities, which constitute the 'raw material' that we can subsequently examine, organise and refine in a more critical and analytical way.

The name of the game works equally well in the arts and the sciences. So for instance when children are asked to write a story, strategies that allow them to have lots of ideas to begin with will be most useful. The decisions they make as to which ideas to use (and why) come later. Similarly the 'creative flow' when writing should not be inhibited by more analytical concerns about the technical accuracy of the sentences themselves – the editing and refining at the word and sentence level can be done later – which is what drafting is all about. (This process applies particularly to less experienced writers. Children who are trying to get everything right *as they write* will find the writing process more difficult and frustrating and far less enjoyable. More experienced writers will tend to produce more polished work at the outset, since the rules will have become embedded in their minds, though reviewing and reworking is of course usually still necessary.)

Similarly, asking children to suggest hypotheses in science to account for an observed phenomenon (such as why the moon has phases or why thunder follows lightning) is essentially a creative act. Ideas brainstormed at this stage are not judged or tested yet since the purpose is to gather a range of possibilities to investigate later. Another useful maxim in this context is 'to have our best ideas we need to have lots of ideas'. Deciding which idea or ideas are 'best' (i.e. those that most closely account for the facts) forms the more experimental/analytical stage of the scientific process.

All this said, the bedrock of our thinking is our natural curiosity: with very little prompting we feel the need to find out more. The basic skills necessary to satisfy that curiosity are noticing and questioning, which find focus and direction through our amazing resources of memory and imagination. As we discover more we become more 'informed', which is to say we actively form greater meanings and understandings about the world, which in turn enrich our store of memories and empower our imagination to conceive of further, greater possibilities.

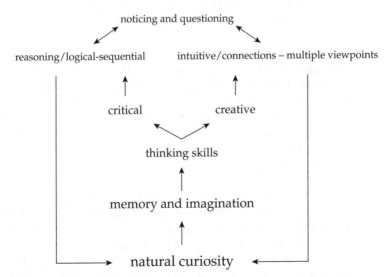

Figure 0.1 Natural curiosity

Core principles for developing thinking/problem solving

We've already touched on the notion that developing thinking depends heavily on children feeling safe to have ideas and being allowed to work out solutions for themselves. These are two key elements of the ethos for thinking that needs to be established in the classroom (if it is not already there). The ability to think independently and actively goes hand in hand with a certain degree of self-confidence and raised self-esteem in the children. Such an ethos – the spirit within which good thinking happens – can be created in a number of ways:

Making the thinking explicit

This means that as far as possible we feed back to the child what has gone on in his mind based on his verbal responses, facial expressions and so on. This is not as difficult as it sounds. Simply saying something like, 'Well done, you've given us three clues that you've noticed as to why you think the picture was taken in the autumn' helps all the children in the class to understand the structure of inferential thinking – searching for further clues to support an idea or insight triggered by a first observation. Making children's thinking explicit in this way very quickly gives them the 'how to' approach we wish to cultivate.

Value it before you evaluate

Children are still learning (aren't we all!) and learn to think most effectively when their thinking – the effort they put into it as well as its outcomes – is valued. This doesn't mean that we automatically have to agree with their opinions or leave shaky reasoning uncorrected, but it does mean that appreciating their contribution because they've bothered to have a go will act as an encouragement for them to keep trying.

This point also raises the important distinction between achievement and attainment. If a child puts a lot of time and effort into thinking an idea through then his achievement is commendable even if ultimately the idea itself is radically altered or even discarded. Similarly, if a child who is usually a reluctant writer finds the motivation from somewhere to write a two-page story, even if the work is largely illegible and full of inaccuracies, that child's achievement merits praise even if the attainment score we must give is low.

Thinking time

The idea of giving children time to think is very familiar now in many classrooms. Most obviously it takes the form of us as teachers resisting the temptation to jump in with ideas of our own or with the right answer. As children come to know more about how to think, long silences following a question will tend to indicate reflectiveness rather than the fact that they haven't got a clue. By the same token, during a discussion or an idea-generating game it's always worth reinforcing the fact that children can ask for more thinking time. Telling the class that 'It's OK to say that you need more time to think' is very reassuring to the children and is a right (rather than a privilege) that is rarely abused. I usually find that when I allow children thinking time instead of putting them under pressure to answer straight away, they come back shortly afterwards with a considered response.

The right to change your mind

An old saying has it that 'four things come not back; the spoken word, the sped arrow, the past life, and the neglected opportunity'. That said, whatever words have been spoken children should be able to amend their ideas, opinions, judgements etc. in light of further thought: this is actually a key element of P4C – developing philosophical enquiry with children. With my particular interest in creative writing, I encourage children to 'show their workings': rather than scribble out a word or sentence so it can't be read, I ask instead that perceived mistakes simply have a line put through them so that I can see the 'before' and 'after' choices and thus gain some insight into the child's reasoning. Also, before marking their work I sometimes ask children to review it and make margin notes about anything they would do differently if they were writing it now. Children are often very insightful about how they would go about improving their work – and this of course creates another opportunity to value their ideas.

A community of thinkers

The well-worn idea that 'we're all in this together' certainly applies in the thinking classroom. Though outside forces may invoke us to cultivate 'the brightest and the best' so that we might 'run and fight in the global race', at heart surely we would ideally like to see all children enjoy their learning, support and celebrate each other's efforts, take pride in their achievements and endeavour to fulfil their own individual potentials. As such the most powerful thinking classroom contains a community of thinkers, where being better than someone else is less important than being the best that you can be and where individual contributions are invited and appreciated because being an effective thinker means taking an interest in and respecting what other people think.

Thoughts and feelings are linked
Everything said so far underpins the fact that our thoughts and feelings are connected. This is a simple notion to state but the idea has many implications. As I've mentioned, the most immediate of these is that children will become better thinkers when they feel *safe* to think and when their ideas are encouraged and valued. This in turn implies the notion that to encourage means 'to give courage to'; it is something that often enough we need to supply to those children who don't bring it with them into the classroom for themselves. (Interestingly the word courage has etymological links with 'heart', which reinforces the thinking–feeling synergy that I'm talking about.) So in a thinking classroom children are learning not just to exercise greater choice and control when it comes to using their imaginations, but are also learning to deal more capably with unhelpful or negative emotions in the face of setbacks or other difficulties – hence the section on problem solving and emotional resourcefulness.

USING THE BOOK

As in my companion volume *Jumpstart! Creativity* (2007), the activities in this book can be used individually or in a progressive sequence: they have been organised to facilitate either approach. A game might constitute a 'mind warm-up' to jumpstart a lesson and get the children into learning mode, or could form the substance of the lesson itself. Linked activities can be interwoven with your own programmes of work across a range of subjects or serve as the basis for a short course in developing thinking in its own right.

I have tried to ensure that the activities are of practical value and applicable across a wide age and ability range, and that they can be launched with minimal preparation. Some of them are extensions of ideas found in *Jumpstart! Creativity* (ibid.) while others are new to this book.

Finally, I would encourage you to adapt and refine any ideas you find here to suit your own particular needs and requirements. Not only will this make the book a more useful resource, but it will also give good experience in the kinds of thinking you are aiming to teach the children!

CHAPTER 1

Jumpstart the problem-solving attitude

The *Concise Oxford English Dictionary* defines a problem in the following ways:

- a doubtful or difficult question or task
- a thing which is hard to understand
- a proposition in which something has to be constructed
- an enquiry starting from given conditions to investigate a fact, result or law.

Roget's Thesaurus adds to the concept by offering a number of synonyms and closely related ideas: enigma, difficulty, worry.

What all of these have in common is the fact that problems by their very nature require sustained active engagement from those who are set the task of trying to solve them. An almost universal characteristic is that problems are difficult and that hurdles, setbacks and disappointments are commonly part of the process. Added to that there is always lurking in the background the possibility of failure. As such, in developing children's thinking and problem-solving capabilities we must from the outset seek to establish in them the 'problem-solving attitude', which embodies features such as:

- determination: the ability to sustain a fixed intention;
- resilience: the tendency to 'bounce back' in the face of complications or failures;
- creativity: the ability to generate multiple strategies that may resolve the issue;

- flexibility: the willingness to tolerate ambiguity and uncertainty during the problem-solving process. Linked to this of course are the attributes of patience and tolerance;
- playfulness, which supports all of the above and makes problem solving an enjoyable pastime. Of course, when problems are serious and personal it is difficult to be 'playful' in any light-hearted sense, though maintaining a positive attitude allows for clearer thinking and helps one to access and exploit resources of inner strength.

Effective and creative thinkers are recognised by a developing expertise, both in terms of the skills necessary to tackle problems and by a sound knowledge base within the areas where the challenges occur. Good problem solvers also tend to be motivated primarily by the interest and endeavour inherent in the problems themselves, rather than by external factors such as impressing people, meeting deadlines and targets or (in the 'world of work') making money. Having said that, people who are good at solving problems do attract credit, praise and other benefits.

One way of beginning to instil the problem-solving attitude in children (or to strengthen it where it already exists) is through the use of quotes and stories of people who have overcome adversity and found success. These are readily available on the internet and form a useful focal point for lessons/topics in every subject area. Two of my own favourite quotes are:

> It's not that I'm so smart, it's just that I stay with problems longer.
>
> Albert Einstein

> We do these things not because they are easy, but because they are hard.
>
> John F. Kennedy
> (when in 1961 he pledged that America would put
> a person on the moon by the end of the decade)

BLOCKS ON THINKING

We've already touched on some of the characteristics of people who are creative and who display the problem-solving attitude. These amount to 'specific observable behaviours' – SOBs – which constitute evidence of effective thinking as robustly as children's written (or otherwise recorded) outcomes of the challenges they've tackled.

By the same token children's behaviour will also clue us in to what has been called the 'safeguarding self'. Children who usually do not relish challenge and wish to stay safe when it comes to solving problems will tend to:

- be cautious rather than curious;
- stick to what they know rather than enjoy striking out into new areas;
- rely more on others rather than express independent ideas and views;
- regard mistakes as weaknesses and failures rather than learning opportunities;
- be overly serious rather than excited, playful and determined in the face of problems;
- be rigid and limited in their thinking rather than flexible, exploratory and experimental;
- keep feelings about learning tasks private rather than express aspirations, confusions, difficulties and disappointments.

Teacher task: The 'problem-solving curriculum' is more process based than content based. Or perhaps it would be more accurate to say that curriculum content forms the raw material out of which challenges and problems are constructed (there's much more on this point throughout the book). As you establish the problem-solving classroom, consider reviewing the behaviour of your children in light of the characteristics noted above.

(You may well find, incidentally, that the safeguarding child is just as likely to be academically very able as not. Sometimes 'bright' children seek to maintain their status by sticking to what they know, avoiding risks and relying mainly upon remembered knowledge, i.e. right answers, rather than trying to make fresh connections.)

Of course it is important to structure programmes of work so that children feel they can move away from their comfort zones into areas where the problem-solving attitude has a chance to grow – the so-called 'stretch zone' where the conceptual sophistication of information and the difficulty of tasks lies at the edge of children's current capabilities. Simply put, this means enabling children to move beyond their existing knowledge and understanding.

In creating the bridge between what is familiar and safe, and what is new and more challenging note in yourself and the children commonly recognised blocks on effective thinking. These include:

- an emphasis on the right answer (especially that it should be arrived at quickly);
- an insistence that the rules (in whatever context) should be followed rigidly;
- dismissing out of hand ideas that seem irrational, off the wall etc.;
- avoiding ambiguity and sticking to what is known, established, correct etc.;
- a chronic belief (carried by both teachers and children) that children are not creative;
- a tendency to judge ideas as being odd, foolish, wrong and so on.

Here are some further ideas for cultivating the problem-solving attitude.

- Change unhelpful metaphors. Metaphors reflect the way we perceive reality. If as teachers we talk of a writer's 'block' then children will think of the phenomenon in that way. Children might well feel and act differently if a writer's block was reframed as a writer's 'chance to daydream'.

In this context, 'blocks' to thinking could be regarded as 'opportunities for change'. Similarly in talking of 'stretch' zones we evoke the whole physical vocabulary of education, where children are also pushed, pulled, driven, drilled, fighting, running and grouped into 'cohorts' (originally a unit of the Roman army). As a thought experiment, consider replacing these terms with the vocabulary of gardening: cultivating, nurturing, tending, flourishing, seeds, fruits, cycles, organic, natural and so on.

- Dedicate some display space to stories of endeavour, enterpreneurship and resilience.

    As a writer I'm uplifted by accounts of how famous books were initially rejected. The first Harry Potter novel was turned down 12 times; Zane Grey, writer of Westerns, was told that he had 'no business being a writer and should give up' (it is estimated that over 250 million copies of his books are currently in print); Beatrix Potter's *The Tale of Peter Rabbit* was rejected so many times that she decided to self-publish, producing a modest print run of 250 copies that went on eventually to sell over 45 million copies (see www.literaryrejections.com).

    Similar examples exist in the world of science. Thomas Edison for instance apparently tested over 6,000 different materials to find a substance suitable for an electric lightbulb. By the time he died in 1931 he had patented nearly 2,000 inventions that he'd created.

- Celebrate what children already do well. Consider inviting children to make presentations of their hobbies and interests to the class. Use these as opportunities to encourage children to listen well, take an interest, ask open questions and connect new ideas and facts to what they already know.

    Time and budget permitting, invite professionals from different fields into the school to talk about the passion they have for their chosen careers.

THE THINKING LADDER

In 1956, the educational psychologist Benjamin Bloom and colleagues developed a theory of 'learning domains' to help promote higher forms of thinking in education over and above the relatively low order skill of simply remembering facts (rote learning). The three domains are: Cognitive (mental skills), Affective (growth in feelings or emotional areas) and Psychomotor (manual or physical skills).

Bloom's original categories in the cognitive realm are: knowledge, comprehension, application, analysis, evaluation and synthesis. These range from relatively simple kinds of thinking that require less understanding to more advanced thinking that demands fuller understanding and manipulation of ideas. In the mid-1990s Lorin Anderson, who was one of Bloom's students, renamed the categories to reflect the notion that they are essentially active processes rather than just labels. Anderson also argued that 'creating' (synthesis) should replace evaluation as the top rung of the ladder. Using the more recent terminology, Bloom's taxonomy or levels of thinking are shown in Figure 1.1.

In using the taxonomy to structure learning tasks it is worth bearing a few points in mind:

- Although the categories are often thought of as being hierarchical (like a ladder), progress from remembering to creating is not necessarily linear. Also, many tasks and challenges will require children to do several kinds of thinking.
- It is wrong to assume that younger or 'less able' children will be unable to engage in more complex kinds of thinking. Although we all learn to think in a more sophisticated way as we mature, even very young children will analyse ideas and make connections between them in their endeavour to make sense of the world.

In this context the educationalist John Abbott has said that young children in particular have 'the wonderful ability to create naïve theories of everything'. A powerful argument can be made that at its heart education is (or should be) about cultivating that creative energy while enriching the knowledge base and experiences of children so that ultimately they can generate more *informed* theories of everything – or at least within those areas where their interests and aptitudes lie.

Category	Key words/Activities
Remembering – being able to recall previously learned information	define, describe, find, identify, know, label, list, match, memorise, name, outline, recall, recite, recognise, reproduce, select, state, summarise, tell
Understanding – being able to comprehend and interpret ideas	convert, defend, distinguish, edit, estimate, explain, extend, generalise, give an example, infer, interpret, paraphrase, predict, restate, rewrite, summarise, translate
Applying – being able to use a concept in a new classroom task/situation and more broadly in life	change, compute, construct, demonstrate, discover, manipulate, model, modify, operate, predict, prepare, produce, relate, show, solve, use
Analysing – being able to separate ideas/information into their component parts: understanding the structure/organisation of presented material	break down, categorise, classify, compare, contrast, deconstruct, differentiate, discriminate, distinguish, identify, illustrate, infer, investigate, outline, relate, represent in a different way (e.g. diagram), select, separate
Evaluating – being able to make considered judgements (including knowing the value of an idea, object etc)	appraise, compare, conclude, contrast, criticise, critique, defend, describe, discriminate, evaluate, explain, grade, interpret, justify, prioritise, rate, recommend, relate, summarise, support
Creating – being able to put parts together into a new whole with a focus on the value of the new idea, meaning, structure etc	argue (the case for), categorise, combine, compile, compose (in words, music etc), construct, devise, design, explain, extrapolate, formulate, generate, imagine, invent, modify, organise, plan, rearrange, reconstruct, refine, relate, reorganise, revise, rewrite, summarise, tell, write

Figure 1.1 Bloom's taxonomy

Another important point arising from this concerns the notion of originality. An idea that a child has just created (i.e. a new link that she has made between previously separate pieces of information) may be obvious and commonplace to us, but is still original to the child and should be valued as such.

In applying Bloom's ideas to thinking/problem solving challenges, consider:

- having the taxonomy prominently displayed in the classroom together with the key words that help to define and describe the categories of thinking;
- using these terms as part of the children's growing 'vocabulary of thinking' so that they will increasingly be able to associate the different kinds of thinking with the tasks that you give them (this also helps to reinforce the principle of 'making the thinking explicit' as a strategy for developing thinking);
- designing questions that require children to think in the various ways highlighted by Bloom. Make use of the key words in Figure 1.1 to do this;
- emphasising the children's thinking when you mark their work. This again makes the thinking explicit. One way of doing this is to use images to represent different kinds of thinking: a question mark to represent asking; two question marks facing one another to represent asking a question about a question; a magnifying glass to represent investigating, and so on.

You might consider getting the children to come up with ideas for suitable images. Ideally these can be quickly and easily drawn, but another option is to print them on sheets of stickers to stick on the children's work.

4Cs THINKING

This handy idea helps to establish and maintain an enjoyable 'thinking environment' which will nourish the core skills of noticing and questioning in the children. The four Cs of thinking are: creative, critical, caring and collaborative.

Creative thinking

At its heart creative thinking consists of making fresh connections and looking at things in as many different ways as possible. These attributes are evident in most of the activities throughout this book, but you can also highlight them with quick kickstarter activities such as these:

- Show the class an ambiguous image such as those in Figure 1.2 and ask, 'What could this be? What does it remind you of?' Brainstorm ideas for a few minutes (i.e. collect ideas without judging or otherwise commenting on them).

Figure 1.2 Ambiguous shapes

Here you can use competitiveness as a positive force: next time you run the activity mention to the class the number of ideas they thought of last time and suggest that they could probably do better now.
- A linked activity is to present the class with a word like 'set' or 'good' or 'right' and ask the children to think of sentences that use those words in as many different ways as possible. With a word like 'good' in particular follow up the game by thinking of more precise adjectives – so rather than a good book, an exciting book etc. This activity also helps children to appreciate the idea that the meaning of a word is often dependent upon the context in which it is used.

Tip: You can focus the 'what could it be' game into different topic areas by showing the class antique objects, scientific instruments, unusual machines, features of the landscape and so on.

Critical thinking

This requires the analysis and assessment of ideas; skills that are honed through discussion and constructive argument (among other ways). Present the class with suitable statements and ask the children whether they agree or disagree. Proverbs are a useful starting point.

So, for example, using 'A fool and his money are soon parted':

- Clarify the meaning of the proverb and any significant words (in this case 'fool').
- Ask the children to indicate whether they agree or disagree with the statement.
- Ask for examples in each case. So one child might say that someone who spends money gambling rather than buying necessities is a fool. Another child might say that a person can be foolish in one way (not eating healthily for example) but be sensible when it comes to money.
- Test the veracity of the proverb in light of the children's ideas. Do the children still feel the same way if we say 'A fool and his money are always soon parted' or 'A wise person and his money are never parted'?
- Use ideas that open up the discussion. These can be other proverbs that are linked to the first one, or statements that you have made up, for example: 'A fool in love will soon have no money' or 'Once a fool, always a fool'.

Tip: Highlight the use of extremes such as 'always', 'never' etc. and the seductive quality of generalisations to elicit a 'knee jerk response'. A great example I came across is 'Drinking milk is good for you'. Everyone in the class immediately agreed apart from one child who pointed out that drinking milk is not good for you if you have a food intolerance to it.

Playing with proverbs provides opportunity for children to practise basic skills of discussion such as *really* listening to what's being said; feeling that their own ideas will be listened to and appreciated; having the right to change their mind (and feeling comfortable about that); developing greater control over their own feelings, so that even if they passionately disagree with someone they can challenge the point itself whilst respecting the person who holds the opposing belief.

Clearly such 'discussion skills' serve as a context for caring/ collaborative discussion and pave the way for more searching philosophically oriented enquiries (which we'll touch on later).

Caring thinking

So-called 'caring thinking' readily engages the emotions and so creates the opportunity for children to be more aware of their feelings as they learn strategies for enhancing positive emotions and modifying negative ones – there's more on this in the section on 'The problem-solving process' below and in Chapter 5 in the section 'Emotional resourcefulness'.

Another aspect of caring thinking is to be aware of other people's feelings. To do this often means that a child must draw on her own experiences but also make the leap of imagination that puts her in someone else's shoes to appreciate how the world looks from another perspective. For example:

- Show the class a picture of a busy street scene. Tell the children that on the count of three they must imagine going into the picture and being part of it. Ask them to imagine people, objects and buildings that are out of the frame, e.g. by imagining they can walk to the end of the street and turn a corner.
- Run the activity again but this time ask the children to pretend that they are someone else – a homeless person, an elderly person, a pickpocket etc. What thoughts and feelings do they notice now?

Tip: This is a quick and effective way to help children generate characters for stories, but it also develops empathy – the ability to see the world from someone else's viewpoint.

Another aspect of caring thinking concerns itself with morals and values. We'll look at this later but useful starter activities include:

- Looking at the concept of value and discussing its various meanings. How can value be different from cost? Think of things that are valuable in different ways, for instance a rare painting, someone's loyalty, a sunset, a wad of banknotes.
- 'Do the right thing'. Hold brief brainstormings/discussions on what would be the 'right' thing to do in a given situation: finding someone's wallet in the street; noticing a burglar breaking into a house; realising your friend is cheating in a test; seeing that a neighbour is neglecting their pet cat. Get the children to come up with further examples to explore.

Collaborative thinking

Collaborative thinking creates a context that brings the other kinds of thinking together. The immediate benefits of collaborative thinking are that it reinforces the idea of a 'community of thinkers', helps children to develop a sense of their own achievement that grows out of their individual contribution to the common goal, and helps them to understand and value the contributions of others. Try the following activities:

- Ask children to reflect on what personal qualities they could bring to a group or team project.
- Put their insights into practice. Split the class into groups and challenge them with a team task. This might be small-scale, local and topical (how can we get all the children in the school through the canteen at lunchtime more effectively?) or something more broadly based (what can be done about coastal erosion and property damage from storms?).
- As part of the project, encourage the children in each group to assign themselves tasks, as far as possible in line with the personal qualities they bring to the activity.

THE FIRST SNATCHED THOUGHT

The mind works quickly. If you've run the 'what could it be' game (**pp. 31–32**) you'll know that many children respond instantly to the prompt. The speed at which thinking occurs can be a great benefit if it is tempered by:

- tolerance of ambiguity and uncertainty: being comfortable in the face of a puzzle, problem or mystery and not feeling you need to have all the answers right away;
- withholding judgement and criticism of your own ideas and those of others, especially at the outset when the idea has not been explored. In my view it is a good idea to put a blanket ban on the phrase 'I know this might sound stupid but...' since it means that the child has already evaluated her idea negatively before even telling you what it is!;
- metacognition: the ability to notice and manipulate one's own thoughts. This is a key skill which involves being able to internalise the conscious point of attention and maintain concentration;
- allowing the creative flow of ideas to happen. One common inhibitor of creative thinking is trying too hard coupled with over-reliance on conscious (linear-sequential) thinking. Creative ideas/insights/fresh connections are generated mainly at a subconscious level. Once you have consciously identified a problem or set a thinking task, while maintaining a clear intention that an outcome will occur, stand back and let your mind get on with the job. In other words, don't stand in your own light.

Snatching at a first thought is not only allowable but necessary during a brainstorming session, in line with the principle of having lots of ideas in order to have your best ideas. (Some politically correct individuals prefer to call the activity 'thought showers' or 'ideas cascades'.) The point of a brainstorming session is to generate a wealth of raw material that can be explored and tested subsequently.

Educationally brainstorming has a number of other benefits. It:

- is inclusive insofar as every child has an open invitation to participate;
- is non-judgemental and non-competitive, serving as a platform for further collaborative thinking and learning to occur;
- helps to develop metacognition and the other aspects of effective thinking mentioned above;

- provides a context for the important principle of valuing every child's ideas – valuing thinking before the ideas themselves are evaluated.

To run a brainstorming session:

1 Define and agree on your objective/clearly identify the problem to be solved.
2 Set a time limit for the brainstorming itself.
3 Note all the ideas offered. As a facilitator do not allow any discussion, analysis or criticism of the ideas at this stage.
4 After the 'ideas cascade' has run its course, categorise/condense/combine/refine the ideas in terms of their usefulness to the solution or outcome.

    Tip: All ideas are potentially useful. Make a box available in the classroom and call it 'the treasure box of ideas'. Any ideas that are not used can be placed in here. Discarded ideas from different sessions can be put into marked envelopes which then go into the box.

5 Prioritise the ideas you've selected to fulfil the outcome to see if they do the job. Further refining and modifying might be needed at this stage.
6 Agree a plan of action in applying the ideas and monitor results.

There are times when snatching at a first thought becomes a habit (what Edward de Bono calls a 'routine' thinking skill). In other words the mental technique is used in a variety of contexts whether or not it is appropriate or effective. One common example is in children's creative writing where some children just grab at the first idea that comes into their mind and build it into the work. In a sense this is letting the creative flow happen and can be useful if a child gets 'stuck' during writing. In this case the technique is being used selectively. However, the first thoughts are not always the best thoughts (hence the notion of redrafting). That said, it is possible to *control* the creative flow of ideas as they happen; to be able to discriminate between ideas as they occur. Hence, writing can be spontaneous and relatively polished. We will look at this further in the next section.

LETTING YOUR IMAGINATION RUN AWAY WITH YOU

A 'runaway' imagination is of little use. The capacity to generate ideas becomes much more useful when used in conjunction with the developing ability to control the creative flow and to some extent select and modify ideas as they become conscious.

A runaway imagination shows itself commonly in children's writing, where the work amounts largely to a string of 'snatched first thoughts' and a tendency for the writer to overuse the weird, wild and wacky in a story. An imagination that is not well controlled also has an effect on how someone reacts emotionally; this being a case of letting your *feelings* run away with you. The ability to notice and modify unhelpful/problematic emotions (and to purposefully select positive ones) is a key feature and benefit of being more 'emotionally intelligent'. We'll explore this more fully later in the book.

For now, try these activities with your children as a way of giving them greater control of their imaginations:

- Ask children to examine an object then close their eyes and imagine it in as much detail as they can. The activity works best if the class is split into small groups. Give each group a different object and encourage the children to discuss what they notice about it in their imaginations – size, shape, colours, textures, weight, sounds and smells (if any). Practise the technique regularly and progressively increase the time you ask the children to concentrate on their mental image.
  Tip: Some children will create more vivid mental images if they can 'mould' the imagined object in their hands.
- Develop the technique by having the children switch objects two or more times during the concentration period. The game is easier if the objects are linked in some way; so, for example, a marble, a ping pong ball, a snooker ball, a tennis ball, a football.
- Allow the children to smell/taste different foods (be aware of allergies, intolerances and personal preferences) then ask them to imagine these as vividly as possible.
  Tip: This is a good opportunity to introduce or revisit similes and metaphors and practise adjective use.

- Show the class the opening scenes of a movie and subsequently ask the children to recreate these in their imaginations.
- Ask the class to imagine a scene such as a busy street, playground, shopping centre etc. Then tell them to enlarge something, make something smaller, take something away, add something. (This acts as a precursor to the Merlin Game on page **25**.)
- Use a similar imagined scene but instruct the children that if they are seeing it 'through their own eyes', to instead float out of their bodies and look at themselves from a third-person perspective. If they do this by default, ask them to look at the scene from a first-person point of view, i.e. through their own eyes.

Use guided visualisations of increasing length to develop children's ability to internalise their awareness, enrich the detail of imagined scenarios and progressively prolong their concentration span.

Guided visualisations incorporate flexibility within a structure. That is to say, they are not as vague as 'Imagine your journey from home to school', but are not overly prescriptive either. Begin by choosing something the children have all experienced, say the layout of the school. Take them on an imagined tour by making a series of statements with 'thinking gaps' in between. So, 'Walk out of the classroom and turn right... Go into Mrs X's room and have a good look round... Choose some small object you can take away with you. Put it in your pocket. Leave the room and take the next left turn...' and so on.

- Write a statement on the board such as, 'They shook hands but only Bowman was smiling'. Give each child a large sheet of paper and ask him/her to write the statement in the middle, then to notice what the sentence conjures up in their imagination and to make notes on the sheet.
- Read a few paragraphs from a story. Split the class into pairs and ask each pair of children to talk about how they imagined that scene differently.

Incidentally, I hope it goes without saying that reading or telling stories to the class on a regular basis greatly enhances the skills we've been looking at – and it's very enjoyable too!

- Ask the children to close their eyes and imagine carrying out some ordinary activity like preparing a salad, making a cup of tea, packing a schoolbag etc. Where something has a definite sequence of steps the children must imagine these in the right order.

- Ask the children to imagine a sporting activity. The particular sport can vary from child to child but preferably should be one that they enjoy. Regardless of how good a child is at his chosen sport, ask him to imagine that he can do it brilliantly well. The visualisation should be as rich and as exact as possible, including precise physical movement and the feelings that emerge during the act.

In this context, neuroscientists have shown that *imagining* performing an activity causes the same networks of brain cells to fire as when that activity is carried out in reality. Also, as an activity is imagined nerve impulses travel from the brain and cause muscle fibres in the body to twitch. In the world of NLP (neuro-linguistic programming) this is called 'training the neurology' (put 'using the imagination in sport' into a search engine for some of the astonishing outcomes of practising this).

The idea of 'letting your imagination run away with you' distinguishes between the imagination and 'you'. As well as being an interesting philosophical point, this highlights the notion that 'we' are potentially the masters of our imaginations and need not be its victims. I tell children that the imagination is like a horse: it is more powerful than they are – but they are the riders.

REALLY LISTENING

I'm sure that no one in education doubts the value of listening skills in learning. A skill has been defined as 'an idea put into practice repeatedly', so in the same way that thinking skills amount to a raft of strategies for showing children *how* to think, listening skills are developed by a variety of strategies for showing children how to listen (above and beyond telling them to 'pay attention and listen').

Here are some ideas:

- Ask the children to sit quietly and either close their eyes or stare at a blank area on the table or a wall. Instruct them to listen to the loudest sound they can hear (this may be people talking in a neighbouring classroom, traffic passing by etc). Then ask them to listen out for the quietest sound they can detect (this might be their own breathing or a breeze blowing outside). Ask them now to relax and just let all the sounds around come into their minds; just listen without having any particular thoughts about what they hear.

  Tip: Some children find it difficult to 'sit quietly'. In this case, practising controlled breathing, relaxation techniques or some physical movement before starting the quiet session can help.

- Play instrumental music regularly to the class. There are various ways of utilising this as a listening session: As children listen, ask them to raise their hands when they hear high notes, lower their hands when there are low notes; move their hands apart when the tempo slows, bring their hands together when the tempo quickens, etc.

  - Say to the children, 'If this music was a person, what would that person be like?' This would include physical appearance, voice, personality and lifestyle. A variation of this visualisation technique is to imagine that the music is a landscape or a cascade of colours.
  - As music plays, ask the children to listen out for particular instruments.

- Reassure children that it's OK for them to ask you or their peers if they don't understand something that has been said. Any of us can easily 'tune out' when what's being said sails over our heads.

- Point out that interrupting or talking over someone is not only ill-mannered but can lead to misunderstandings, false assumptions and jumping to the wrong conclusion.

- Set quickfire listening tasks. Read a short extract that mentions three (or however many) numbers and ask children to give you their total when you've finished. There are endless variations of this idea. How many different names are mentioned in the extract? How many times was the word 'and' mentioned?

- Cultivate the habit of children restating what someone has said to ensure a) that they've really listened and b) that they've interpreted the idea correctly.

- Help children to develop a 'signal' or trigger that they can use to get into listening mode. In NLP this is called an anchor – a link between a desired behaviour and a consciously controlled prompt. In many classrooms the idea is already used in the form of the teacher initiating a clapping game that the children then copy as they stop talking and listen; or putting up your hand as a signal for children to do the same as they pay attention. Anchors can also be individual; but the important point is that children develop the wherewithal to use their anchor and become aware that they are actively listening to what the speaker is saying.

As necessary, make the learning environment conducive to better listening by: cutting down on distractions; previewing learning sessions with keywords and/or summaries of what will be said; dampening the tendency for children to complete someone else's idea (sometimes out of a wish to help them along); and holding your own thoughts about what is being said in abeyance until the speaker has finished.

THE PROBLEM-SOLVING PROCESS

Various ideas about how best to undertake the 'problem-solving process' have been put forward over the years, and while there are a number of definite steps or 'phases' involved in finding solutions, it is important to bear in mind that:

- in reality (and in most cases) problem solving is not a rigidly linear or formulaic activity. The different phases often overlap or indeed a great solution can emerge suddenly as an insight 'out of the blue' – the 'Eureka moment' we've touched on elsewhere;
- solving problems most effectively utilises both conscious (analytical) and subconscious (information assimilating) resources. The key elements of creative thinking – making connections and looking at things in many ways – often happen subconsciously as a 'disposition' of mind rather than through consciously applied techniques.

Here's a suggested model of how the process can work:

1 *Stimulus.* Creative thinking needs some kind of springboard to jumpstart ideas. This may be a first recognition of the problem itself, a perceived need or something as vague as a feeling (of frustration or 'stuckness', for example). If the problem has already been defined to some extent the stimulus might be a picture, some music, a story; these are not necessarily connected to the problem, but serve to get the creative flow of ideas going.

2 *Exploration.* Creative exploration of the potential of the stimulus often follows. Such potential may be simply to generate further ideas. Again these may not seem to be directly connected to the problem, although they may act as 'pointers' towards possibilities that could be investigated first.

3 *Knowledge.* A robust knowledge base helps to clarify the problem and saves time when it comes to prioritising possible solutions. As Louis Pasteur said, 'Chance favours the prepared mind.' In other words, sudden insights don't usually come out of a vacuum but arise from familiarity with and experience of the area where the problem has occurred.

4 *Research/planning.* Systematic research in the field builds a stronger knowledge base and throws light on previous attempts to solve the problem. This may go hand in hand with actively thinking further about the problem and making the thinking visible through drawings and diagrams, discussions, simulations etc.

5 *Incubation.* Practically this means letting go of the problem and doing nothing for a while. At least, doing nothing consciously. Subconsciously all that has gone before – the first ideas, knowledge, research findings and planning strategies – is being assimilated. This is often the point where sudden insights or breakthroughs occur – so-called moments of illumination when the next step forward or indeed a solution comes to light.

6 Possible strategies for resolution are more likely to emerge, however, than a single clear solution. These are usefully prioritised or 'weeded' at this stage (bearing in mind that a maverick idea might ultimately prove to be the most effective).

7 Putting the solution into practice and then reviewing the results will establish that the problem has been solved or, if not, what else needs to be done to achieve this.

You'll appreciate that this template is framed in very general terms. Subsequent sections of the book will offer more specific examples of problems and tried-and-tested strategies for resolving problems. However, you might want to test out the basic problem-solving process by playing the 'what if' game on page **35**.

DESCRIBING AND DEFINING

The word 'define' comes from Latin and means a boundary or limit and is linked to the word 'definite' which is about setting exact limits. Activities that ask children to frame definitions can be both challenging and engaging. Here are some to try out:

- Take vague words such as nice, good, best etc. and ask children to use them in different sentences, then to suggest a definition of the word based on its use in that sentence. So, in the sentence, 'I read a good book at the weekend', 'good' could mean enjoyable, exciting, informative, scary, funny... Is there a satisfactory general definition of the word 'good'?

  Tip: Words like good are 'slippery' words insofar as precise definitions/meanings are sometimes not made clear.
- Take two words of similar meaning and ask the children to discuss how they differ – annoyance and irritation, for example, or big and large. Exploring subtle distinctions between the meanings of words boosts vocabulary and emphasises the value of precision in communication. (Exploring the exact meanings of words and concepts is a key feature of philosophical enquiry.)
- Explore the etymology of words. Word origins are fascinating in themselves but also show that language is 'plastic'; that the meanings of words can change over time. For example, while 'nice' has become a rather insipid synonym for 'pleasant', the original Latin meaning was 'ignorant'. Looking at where words come from also helps children to make useful connections between terms that at first glance seem to have nothing in common. For instance, 'text' and 'context' are linked with the word 'textiles' from the Latin 'to weave'. Sometimes, as in this case, word origins supply useful metaphors such as spinning a

yarn, losing the thread (of what you were saying), unpicking mistakes, weaving ideas together, the fabric of reality etc.

- Similarities and differences. Split the class into small groups and give each group two objects or pictures of objects that are similar; for instance leaves from two kinds of tree. Ask the groups to write down as many differences between the objects as possible, then to think of a definition that connects them.
- Play the Scootems Game. Show the class the image in Figure 1.3 and challenge the children to define what a scootem is.

Figure 1.3 Scootems

Tip: This game is a little bit sly insofar as the scootems have been drawn deliberately to make any definition elusive. If the children are having difficulty, suggest that some of the scootems are broken or have been modified.

- Link describing and defining to categorising and classifying. Show the class pictures of animals for instance and ask the children how they could be sorted into groups. Compare their decisions with 'official' classification criteria. For example, children might put a bird and a bee into the same category of 'flying creature', but why doesn't this count as a valid category scientifically?
- Compare scientific and poetical descriptions of objects, animals etc. In what sense is the language of poetry 'valid'? Is a poem as 'true' as a collection of facts about, say, the moon?
- Play odd-one-out games, then give them a creative spin by asking the children to find at least one reason why the other items in the group could be the odd one out.

MISTAKES ARE USEFUL

Recognising that mistakes can be useful is an important step forward in developing the problem-solving attitude. When children understand that making mistakes is an inevitable aspect of learning they are in a better position to realise their creative potential and to know that there are different categories or 'varieties' of mistake.

In terms of writing there are a number of strategies you can use to help children look at their mistakes in a more positive way:

- Point out occasions when an error shows an emergent understanding of some technical aspect of writing. For instance if a child writes 'wented' instead of 'went', while the word itself is incorrect he has still demonstrated an awareness of the past tense.
- Ask children to put a line through an error they've made rather than scribbling out a word or phrase so that it cannot be seen. If the child herself spots the mistake, invite her to make a note of how she recognised the error.

- Encourage children occasionally to look back over work they did some months before. Use this as an opportunity to tell them that if they can see ways of improving it then they have obviously developed as writers.
- Point out the distinction between mistakes that happen through a lack of knowledge and those that are changes of mind. The creative ethos incorporates the notion that it is fine to change your mind, and again it is useful for children to make their thinking explicit; to explain what led them to make the change.

Sometimes a mistake leads immediately to a creative insight. For example, during a workshop I was running one girl wrote the word 'onyx' but pronounced it 'oinks' (because she had never actually heard it spoken before). Her embarrassment over the error soon vanished however when she decided to write a story with pigs as the main characters. The title of the story was of course going to be 'Oinks'. Similarly my friend, the writer Douglas Hill, when passing a vegetarian café one time noticed a sign for falafel but saw it as 'fallowfall' and decided that this would make a great title for a novel. When I asked him what the novel would be about he smiled and said, 'I have no idea – yet.'

Another fruitful way of using mistakes is to show children how errors in science have often led to breakthroughs. Indeed, science has been called 'a history of corrected mistakes'. In a very important sense science always proceeds from a position of partial understanding motivated by curiosity and the desire to learn more. Give children examples of the way in which 'failed' experiments led to something useful.

For instance, during the Second World War, while attempting to create a synthetic rubber substitute, James Wright dropped boric acid into silicone oil. The result was a polymerised substance that bounced but seemed to have no useful purpose. However, in 1950, the marketing expert Peter Hodgson saw its potential as a toy and named it Silly Putty. Not only is it fun, Silly Putty also has practical uses. It picks up dirt, lint, and pet hair, can stabilise wobbly furniture, and is useful in stress reduction, physical therapy and medical and scientific simulations. It was even used by the crew of Apollo 8 to secure tools in zero gravity.

An Internet search will quickly throw up many more examples.

Finally, in helping children to have a more positive attitude towards mistakes, allow them to appreciate the difference between excellence and perfection. While it is salutary to want to improve and to excel in some chosen field, a perfectionist attitude can lead to anxiety and, ironically, an aversion to risk taking in case the outcome isn't flawless. As the writer and philosopher Arthur Koestler maintains, what matters is not perfection but the quest for originality and opening up new frontiers.

THE MERLIN GAME

This is a classic technique for generating creative ideas and exploring possibilities. I tell children that Merlin is 'the wizard of our imagination' and that by waving our wand over an idea we can change it in different ways. Those ways are: enlarge, reduce, eliminate, stretch, reverse and substitute – or you can say make bigger, make smaller, take something away, (keep 'stretch' the same), turn something around, change one thing for another.

Demonstrate the technique by taking something the children are familiar with, for instance the story of Cinderella. Begin by listing the 'ingredients' of the tale and tell the children they can use as many of them as they want to once the wand is waved.

So in applying the idea of 'enlarge' to the story we come up with:

- Cinderella's feet get bigger and this makes it harder for the Prince to find her using the glass slipper;
- Cinderella has four ugly sisters (who make life even more miserable for her);
- the ongoing adventures of Cinderella.

In applying the idea of 'reduce' we get:

- writing the tale as a 50-word mini saga;
- the fairy godmother isn't very good at magic (i.e. reducing her ability to help);
- the Prince is actually poor and has paid for the ball on credit.

And so on. Develop the technique by applying it to real-world problems. In one school I visited a class applied the Merlin Game to the problem that due to rising numbers the school hall was no longer big enough for everyone to fit inside. Possible solutions included:

- making the hall bigger;
- taking away one wall and replacing it with a sliding screen;
- televising assemblies. Classes would take it in turns to stay in their classrooms and watch the assembly on the TV;
- 'stretching' assembly time and running the assembly twice to half the school at a time.

SOWING THE SEED

We've already touched on the idea that the roots of creative thinking lie in the subconscious part of the mind. Here, information is assimilated largely outside the realm of our conscious awareness. Connections are made 'behind the scenes'. Such processing – an amazing and incompletely understood phenomenon – happens at the general level of allowing us to make sense of the world, but also occurs in response to particular intentions, expectations and stimuli. Sudden insights and the creative flow of ideas are the result of an ongoing attitude that our mind will 'deliver the goods' coupled with specific techniques for prompting subconscious activity that results in those outcomes. As such, the creative subconscious is as necessary and as valuable as our analytical conscious minds in any problem-solving context.

Here are some techniques for exploiting the wonderful resource of the subconscious:

- Be aware that thoughts and feelings are entangled; that creative insights happen more readily when children have higher self-esteem and a degree of self-confidence in their own potential to achieve. (Specific strategies for these are explored in the section on 'Emotional resourcefulness' in Chapter 5)
- *Seed Thoughts*. These are prompts for the subconscious mind to work towards solutions. In terms of creative writing, this might be a desire for a story to 'come together' in the writer's mind, i.e. to have a more definite idea of the structure of the narrative, or for the writer to learn more about a character or characters, or perhaps for him to have a sense of greater certainty in the direction the story is going. A seed thought then might be a few notes about the plot, characters etc. – an indication of what the writer already knows – linked with the definite intention that very shortly further ideas will pop into mind. As a classroom technique, you might give the title of the story or character names to the class and then say, 'And I'm sure you'll know much more about these when we mention them again tomorrow.'

  Tip: Once the creative seed has been sown, just let the children forget about it. Remember that the work is going on subconsciously; conscious effort and struggle at this stage would be largely counterproductive. Also notice the word 'when' in your instruction. This acts as a presupposition of success. Subconsciously the children will register your confidence in and high expectations of their ability to carry out the task.

  It may well be that children will begin to have further ideas around the given task before you revisit the topic. Advise them if that happens just to jot down what comes to mind but not to struggle to write more once the ideas stop flowing naturally.
- *Notes to self.* Ask the children to imagine that their lives are like a path. At this moment they find themselves at a position some way along it. Ask them to write notes to their younger selves that contain snippets of wisdom, messages of encouragement, reassurances that the 'now self' is OK and has learned a lot relative to what he or she knew then. Similarly children can write to their future selves asking for advice and reassurance or (because the 'now self' is in the past as far as the future self is concerned) *specific ideas* about work in progress, or decisions that need to be made.

Obviously we are not talking about actual communication with the future. The point is that we 'know much more than we think we know', so the letter-to-the-future technique is simply an attempt to access more of the mental resources that exist at a subconscious level.

• *Artful vagueness.* This is where you offer the children some vague suggestion or instruction that they will assimilate subconsciously and then 'flesh out' for themselves as insights/solutions become conscious.

Here are some examples of the kind of vague statements I'm talking about:

– Partnerships are to your advantage
– Consider changing direction
– You are about to break into new areas
– Notice what becomes more significant now
– A change of direction brings further results
– The solution is close by
– Look at the whole thing again in a new way

The fact that this sounds like the kind of thing you might read in a newspaper horoscope is no coincidence. Vague, generalised statements are like join-the-dot puzzles: we have a natural tendency to want to connect them and see the whole picture. (In fact, looking at newspaper horoscopes is a good way of gathering further examples of artfully vague statements.)

So if a particular child or group has a problem to solve, ask them to pick out a vague statement at random while they maintain a robust intention that it will lead to practical and effective ideas for its solution.

DECISION TREES

A decision tree is a quick and easy planning tool/visual organiser that helps children to reflect on a number of possibilities when planning a course of action and so dampens the tendency for them to 'snatch at the first thought'. Sometimes children's writing will be full of the first ideas that come to mind and as such the work looks unplanned and is often unoriginal. Considering different options first allows the best or most useful ideas to be chosen and linked in a more robust way. Figure 1.4 shows how a story tree is constructed. It is not necessary for children to think of three options every time, though they can add more if they wish.

Tip: Large sheets of paper will be needed even for a relatively simple tree (a flip chart or sugar paper is good). Also, if the children write their options on sticky notes these can be changed and rearranged as required.

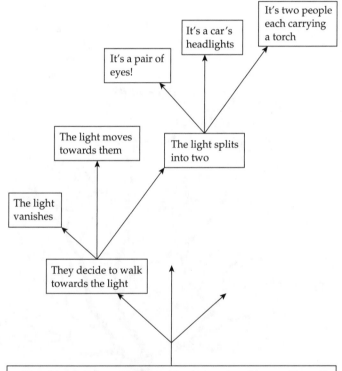

Figure 1.4 Story tree

Topic trees (see Figure 1.5) work in the same way, allowing children (or yourself) to decide how the different elements of a topic are linked and in what order they should be studied or written about.

Decision trees are also useful when teaching children about cause–effect and consequences within the context of emotional resourcefulness and help to familiarise them with the 'if-then' pattern of thinking – 'If I did W then X would be the result. But if I did Y then Z would be the likely result.'

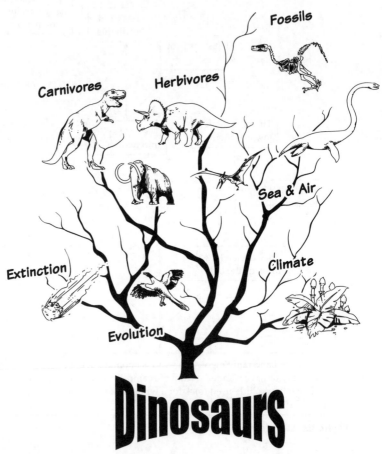

Figure 1.5 Topic tree

POINT OF VIEW

One of the key elements of creative thinking (in any field) is the ability to take a multiple perspective and look at things in different ways. Once this habit is established children will be able to generate even more ideas and put forward their thoughts and opinions with greater confidence. Here are some quick and easy activities for them to try:

- Take a short story and rewrite it from the point of view of a different character; for example, if the hero narrates the story, rewrite it from the villain's perspective.
  Tip: This activity can be varied or extended by rewriting scenes from the point of view of several characters.
- Before a discussion/debate, look at the issue from the point of view that is *opposite* to your own and make a list of ideas that someone arguing against you might use.
- Choose an animal and imagine what the world would look like from the point of view of the animal.
  Tip: Prepare the children for this visualisation by giving them some facts about their chosen creature. Watching natural history programmes is also useful, especially as some of them use footage from cameras actually attached to the animal.
- Imagine you are another person, someone older for example, or someone from another country. What kinds of thoughts and feelings might that person have?
- Imagine you are an alien from outer space and you've just arrived on Earth. You don't know the names for things but are able to describe them. For instance you don't know that a car is called a car, but in sending a report to your home world you can say, 'These Earth creatures move around in little noisy, smelly metal boxes of different colours. The boxes travel on long strips of smooth, dark stony material that form a network across the land. Sometimes there are so many boxes that they come to a standstill and have to wait, occasionally for a long time, before starting to move again.'
- Look at the images in Figure 1.6. What could they be? Think of as many ideas for each one as you can. *Tip:* turn the page upside down to have further thoughts about B, C and D.

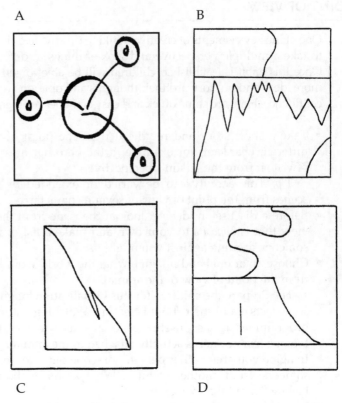

Figure 1.6 What could it be?

- To help in problem solving, imagine that the problem has *already* been solved. Look back from that point of success at what you and your classmates did to get you there.

MENTAL ZOOM TOOL

The philosopher Alfred North Whitehead said that we think in generalities but we live in detail. 'Generalised thinking' as we might call it can become problematic when it obscures the details of our own experience, and especially if the generalisation carries an 'emotional charge' in terms of strong feelings attached to it. Consider the following statements:

> We're worse off now than we have been for years.
> Overall, immigration is a good thing.
> Children today have far less respect for their elders.
> The brightest and the best deserve the greatest rewards.

The first thing to reflect on is whether you reacted emotionally to any of these ideas, and whether the reaction was automatic rather than the result of a considered judgement. Second, notice how the vagueness of the language makes the concepts themselves 'cloudy', such that they raise many questions.

A useful technique to teach children is to ask probing questions about generalised statements. So looking at the first one:

> What do you mean by 'we'?
> In what sense exactly are 'we' worse off?
> In what sense are you using the word 'worse'?
> How many years are you talking about?

The aim of such questioning is to elicit further information. Questions like these often use words like exactly, precisely, in more detail, further explanation etc. If the person who made the generalisation isn't actually present, children can still ask the questions as a way of developing their own analytical abilities while raising their awareness of the slippery nature of some language. A further implicit benefit is that by reflecting on generalisations (rather than just reacting to them), children will become more emotionally resourceful insofar as they are less likely to be influenced by the emotive nature of some statements – such as the language of advertising, political rhetoric and extreme opinions of various kinds.

An extension of the technique of unpicking generalisations is to measure such statements against one's own personal experience, as far as this is possible. This might be described as a 'take as you find' attitude. So if someone tells me that children today have far less respect for their elders, as well as asking probing questions I can think back to times when I've visited schools and decide that, actually no, in my experience this is not the case: most children I meet are friendly and polite.

In a sense generalisations are vague overviews. The techniques above are like a mental zoom tool where we want to focus in on finer detail. The ability to zoom in and out mentally is useful in many ways, not least when it comes to children's writing. Consider the following:

> The princess's eyes were green with little flecks of gold in them.
> The enemy armies were massing, ready to invade.

The first sentence is 'high magnification' of a tiny detail. The second sentence is a low magnification, wide field overview. Encourage children to use the zoom tool flexibly when they write, using overviews to set a scene economically for example, together with vivid details to bring a character or place alive in the reader's imagination.

THE WHILE GAME

This simple activity shows children how the zoom tool works. Begin with a sentence such as 'Jones lay slumped on the sofa.' This gives us a small amount of information but also raises many questions. As a precursor to the game itself you could invite the children to ask probing questions around it.

Now say, 'While Jones was on the sofa, in the flat next door...?' and collect some responses. Use one to take the game forward. Let's say one of the children said, 'Someone was playing music.' Then you say, 'While someone was playing music next door, 20 yards away in the street outside...?' Collect responses and use one to take the game forward.

Each time you use a child's idea, step it farther out in terms of distance. Let's say there was a traffic jam in the street outside. You then say, 'While that traffic jam was happening, two miles away in the middle of town...?' And so on.

As the game progresses we are mentally moving farther away from the little detail of Jones on the sofa, gaining a greater and greater overview of Jones's world.

Help children to understand the game by drawing a series of concentric circles on the board, where each circle represents a stage of the game. Annotate the circles with the children's responses and ask them to contribute further ideas at the appropriate distances.

Finish off the game by playing it in reverse, moving from the outermost circle inwards to Jones still lying slumped on the sofa!

WHAT IF

This is a quick and easy game that serves as a platform for a number of thinking skills across a range of subject areas. First think of a suitable 'what if' and then append these three other questions to it:

1 What would the world be like?
2 What problems could there be?
3 How could we solve those problems?

'What ifs' can be fanciful or related to real-world topics or issues. A fictional focus is useful at the planning stage of story making. For example:

- What if dragons actually existed?
- What if magic was real?
- What if time travel were possible?

The initial brainstorming of ideas adds detail to question 1, whereas exploring question 2 generates ideas related to the conflict and drama that any story needs to include. Thinking of answers to question 3 helps children to devise a suitable resolution for the tale.

A fictional 'what if' can also lead towards practical solutions of real problems. During one workshop the question came up, 'What if people grew normally until they were 30 and then started to shrink, so that by age 60 you were only six inches tall?'

This raised all kinds of issues to do with housing, transport, jobs, town planning, hospitals, the manufacturing industry and others. One boy rightly pointed out that supermarkets for instance would need to be radically redesigned to cater for tiny older people. This led to a further suggestion of shops-on-wheels that would travel to special parts of the town set aside for older people where houses were built smaller and smaller along different streets. This would be necessary because as people aged they would continue to shrink and therefore the houses they lived in would eventually become too big. Out of this came the suggestion that houses for older people could be built in a factory and simply transported to where they were needed. Electricity and water supplies could be laid on in the designated area beforehand and the newly delivered houses simply 'plugged into place'.

This excellent idea created the opportunity for the class teacher to talk about the prefabricated housing that was built after the war, and out of this came further discussion about social housing, land use and the notion of equality in society.

The same class subsequently explored other 'outrageous but relevant' what ifs:

- What if dinosaurs had never become extinct?
- What if gravity disappeared unexpectedly for five minutes every day?
- What if there were two races of humans on Earth and one race could only come out in the day and the other at night?
- What if your mind could go into someone else's body temporarily?

- What if, on the same day every year, people were compelled to tell the truth?

The last two ideas in particular lend themselves wonderfully to philosophical enquiry: discussions about what is a mind or what do we mean by truth could take place either before or after the what if session.

Another important aspect of the activity is that it is usually light hearted. The discussion about people shrinking with age was filled with joking and laughter, even though serious issues were touched upon. The fictional context feels safer for some children, who contribute ideas more readily than if the discussion was about a 'real' topic.

You are also likely to find that a what if starter question prompts children to ask lots of other questions to clarify the situation before the brainstorming begins. Subsidiary questions arising from the shrinking-with-age idea included:

- Do older people shrink at the same rate?
- Do they keep shrinking until they disappear?
- As people shrink do their voices get quieter and quieter until they can no longer be heard?
- Can the shrinking process be stopped or reversed? In which case, can everybody use it? If not, who decides who gets cured?

Incidentally, you'll find that a number of the more outlandish what ifs have been covered in science fiction and fantasy books and films, for instance the classic 1957 sci-fi movie *The Incredible Shrinking Man*, directed by Jack Arnold and based on the Richard Matheson novel. The film would be suitable viewing for Y5–6 (if the children can stand watching it in black and white!).

THE POWER OF OPEN QUESTIONS

I'm sure that no one involved in the education profession can doubt the value of children asking open questions. I devoted a section to questioning techniques in *Jumpstart! Creativity* (2007), the companion volume to this book, but would like to add a few things here:

- It is worth doing a 'question audit' in your classroom. That means noticing what kinds of questions are asked and by whom. As you establish a 'thinking environment' in your classroom you should find increasingly that it's the children who ask the questions (rather than predominantly the adults in the room) and that the questions become progressively more incisive. In other words, closed procedural questions such as, 'Shall I write in pen?' or 'Does this work go in my best book?' will be replaced or at least added to by open questions that have more to do with the knowledge content of the lesson and the thinking habits that you're cultivating.
- Encourage children to restate ideas in their own words. This habit is feedback to you and to them that they've understood the concept, plus it helps to avoid misunderstandings, misinterpretations and confusions. Such restatements often take the form of a question such as, 'So are you saying that...?' or 'Do you mean then that...?'
- Combine offering children straight facts with questions about the topic area that get them to do more thinking for themselves. To help overcome children's common 'fear of the wrong answer' it is worth basing some of your questions on the children's opinions and viewpoints rather than straight recall of subject content.

    Tip: With that in mind, when I trained as a teacher my mentor advised me that 'A good teacher is always prepared to admit "I don't know, but how might we find out?"' Actually this is a very elegant statement because a) it conveys to the child that it's OK not to know all of the answers at that point, b) it invites the child to think creatively (and gives you the opportunity to value that thinking) and c) it reinforces the message that true understanding comes about through asking effective questions rather than just passively accepting answers.
- Play Twenty Questions regularly and inject an element of competition by wondering if the class can improve on their previous best. Occasionally combine the game with an analysis of the questions that have been asked to discover which were the most effective and why.

- Feature a 'question star' (see Figure 1.7) prominently in the classroom as an ongoing visual reminder for children to ask open questions. Consider supplying each child with a question star bookmark to reinforce the habit of questioning.

Figure 1.7 Question star

- Consider making display space for a 'Question of the Week'. Either select a different child or group to think of and post up a really intriguing question, or draw questions at random out of a 'what-I'd-like-to-know-is…' box that children can put questions into at any time. As a child's/group's question is on display, give them a merit badge so that they too are question 'stars' of the moment.
- Show the class a picture like the one shown in Figure 1.8 and play a heads-and-tails game where the children ask yes-or-no questions about it. A yes (heads) answer gives them a definite piece of information on which to base further questions, while a no (tails) answer means they've got to think of another idea. So asking 'Is the woman frightened?' and getting the answer 'no'

means that children have to invent an alternative explanation for her behaviour.

Tip: Increase the challenge of the game by telling the children to think of open questions first and then convert them into closed questions. So 'What is the woman doing?' 'Is she running away from someone?' 'Is the man trying to run her down?' 'Is she really angry about something?' etc. Playing the coin flip game is also a great way of helping children to plan stories.

Figure 1.8 Coin flip

THE LEARNING'S IN THE DETAIL

One of the most obvious and immediate uses of noticing things is to observe and articulate differences. This basic skill can apply in any area of learning and I feel needs to be established as a habit of thought as early as possible. The activity can be light-hearted and does not need to take up much time: spotting differences (and similarities) can be a jumpstart warmup to any lesson:

- Play spot the difference with pictures. In Figure 1.9 there are five differences to notice. Using simple graphics packages, ask children to create their own pairs of subtly different images.

Figure 1.9 Spot the difference

- Change something about your classroom on a regular basis. Begin with obvious changes and make them subtler over time (letting the children know the day before that they will have something to look out for tomorrow). The game can also be played using a selection of objects on a tabletop – rearrange a couple of them, take something away, add something, replace an object with one of a slightly different colour etc.
- Consider giving children observational tasks to do out of school – noticing and writing a brief description of a person, collecting a number of vehicle licence plates (not literally of course), making a list of five things they have never noticed before on the journey from school to home.
- The activity can be extended by giving each child an observation journal. Take the group outside and encourage them to notice what's around – the colours of leaves, the shades of green of the grass, the way clouds drift across the sky, the smell of the air, the particular feeling of the breeze as it blows by, etc.

Focus on one sense at a time. Give children time to notice sights, sounds etc. and to make a brief note of their impressions before moving on to the next focus of attention. Explain that there is no need to write or draw something every time: the primary purpose of the activity is to become more aware of the outdoors and enrich your experience of being there.

Some children may use comparisons spontaneously, but their impressions are useful anyway for introducing or revisiting similes and metaphors.

Back in the classroom, compare children's various impressions of what they noticed. Discuss the language without necessarily judging it. For example, some children might say 'the wind howled around me'. This is a cliché and might not convey a very accurate impression at all, but to help the child to think beyond their 'first snatched thought' you might say 'If the wind had been gentler than that, what word(s) would you use to describe it?'

- Present the class with sentences that are slightly different. Ask children to notice and tell you what they see; they don't need to know the grammatical rule behind the difference at this stage. So: 'Tony borrowed a book from his brother's bookcase' and 'Tony borrowed a book from his brothers' bookcase.' Extend the idea by introducing the notion of bias and 'spin'. For instance, the following sentences are factually the same but might well evoke different emotional responses: '29% of the population are now more optimistic about the economy' and '71% of the population are not more optimistic about the economy.'

- Show the class a prefix or root word and ask the children to create a collection of words that contain it. Then do a dictionary search to check which or if words are etymologically linked.

- Explore differences between synonyms. How is happiness different from joy when you experience those emotions? Do irritation and annoyance feel the same? Extend the activity into the realm of 'emotional intelligence' by encouraging children to notice people's facial expressions and body language.

THE CIRCLE GAME

This is a flexible technique that can serve to introduce or extend children's experience of visual organisers. Give children the circle template shown in Figure 1.10 or ask them to create one of their own. Here are some ways of using it:

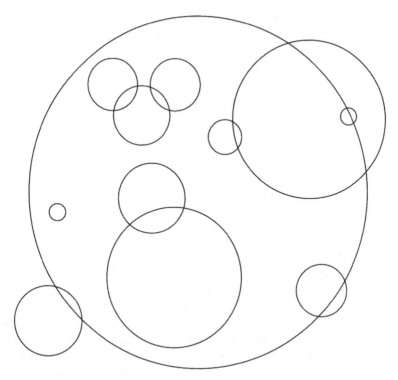

Figure 1.10 Circle game

- Imagine the large circle represents someone's mind and/or personality. The smaller circles represent things that are on that person's mind; the larger the circle, the more that person is thinking about it and the stronger the feelings that are associated with it. Overlapping circles mean that those thoughts and feelings are connected. Circles that extend beyond the edge of the large circle are being expressed by the person verbally and/or through other kinds of behaviour.

   Ask the children to decide what thoughts/feelings the circles stand for and what has been going on in that person's life to account for his 'mental map'. Children can write and draw within the circles to illustrate their ideas.

- Now ask the children to think of one or more events that happen to alter the configuration of the circles. Ask them to draw the new template to reflect the changes in that person's life.
- Split the class into small groups and give each group two of the circle templates that the children have worked on previously. Ask the groups to imagine a situation where the two 'circle people' meet and discuss what the people might say to one another, how they would get on together (or not). Keep the discussion going by giving the groups a 'what if' – what if those people were both in a bank when a holdup happened? What would they do and say?
- Give the groups a circle template where you have previously written in one of the circles. The annotation could be a feeling like envy or kindness or a value like loyalty or selflessness. Ask the groups to think about what the other circles might represent in light of this.
- Use a circle to represent a literary genre, say Fantasy. Other circles inside it stand for the motifs and conventions of the genre; that is the constituent features that help to define and describe the genre. The size of the subsidiary circles represents the importance and/or frequency of that given motif. So, for example, 'dragons' would be a large circle within the main one while 'talking crystals' would be much smaller, since this idea crops up much less often than dragons do in Fantasy tales.

  Used in this way the circle template serves as a device for gathering ideas for and planning a story. Give each child or group a large sheet of paper with the main circle printed on it, plus a collection of smaller circles that can be drawn and written on. Encourage the children to move the smaller circles around as they think about what could happen in their story.

  Tip: This is an example of where subconscious assimilation takes place. Advise the children not to struggle to try and think of ideas; instead say, 'Let the ideas come to you.'
- Challenge the children by asking them how else the circle template could be used. You can give some examples if necessary – for instance, how could the template apply to planning a new school/preparing to colonise Mars/revising for a test/resolving an argument with a friend?

HOW DID IT GO?

As children become more experienced and confident thinkers their own impressions of the quality of the work they do and the effort they've put into it will become more sophisticated and perceptive. Offering them the opportunity to comment on their work reinforces the core principle of 'valuing the thinking' and creates opportunities to talk about determination and resilience as valuable qualities when it comes to fulfilling one's potential.

(Note here that I mean endeavouring to achieve one's personal best. This is not necessarily the same as competing with others and trying to be 'top of the class' or reach some externally imposed level. There is also the distinction to be made between 'achievement' – feeling pleased with the effort made and valuing what's been learned – and 'attainment', which I associate more with comparisons against some general standard.)

Here are some ways of encouraging children to think about their work and performance:

- *The PIN strategy.* This stands for positive, interesting, negative and involves suspending judgement and not jumping to premature conclusions, for instance during a class discussion or an idea-generating session. Rather, children are asked to reflect on these three aspects of an idea and, indeed, actively to look for elements that fit all three categories as far as possible. Once the strategy has been applied as part of an activity, collect PIN responses as material for further discussion and highlight the value of suspending judgement as a thinking skill.
- *Annotated workbooks.* For some of their projects, ask the children to write/draw only on the left hand pages of their books. The right hand pages are to stay blank until the project is finished, when you invite the children to comment on the piece they've completed. Such comments would include noting areas of difficulty and confusion, highlighting parts of the work that the writer thinks have been done well, comparing this piece with others, noting what has been learned and so on. Emphasise that you are not going to judge or mark these comments, but they

will be useful to you in seeing how the child is coming on, and in planning your strategies for future lessons.

- *Reflective diaries.* These are an extension of the annotated workbook. Here children can comment on their lives in general, on their school experiences and progress, or just on particular pieces of work. Rereading their entries will help children to pick out and celebrate strengths and successes and to take positive action with areas of difficulty.
- Encourage the children to share effective strategies and techniques with regard to their learning. So, for example, one child might report that he can spot mistakes more easily in his work if he reads it slowly out loud to himself. Another might suggest making a list of 'words I've learned this week' and finding the opportunity to use them in discussion. Collectively the class can come up with many useful tips that any particular individual may never have thought about.
- Quick check review questions. Encourage children to review particular pieces of work, their progress over a term etc. by the use of some simple review questions:
  - How did it go?
  - What worked well?
  - What could have been better?
  - What did I learn (about the topic and about *how* to learn)?
  - What will I do differently next time?

PRAISE WHERE IT'S DUE

Two of the most powerful motivators for encouraging children to 'have a go' are *quick feedback* and *sincere praise*.

Quick feedback means verifying for the child that he has demonstrated the behaviour you wanted from him; this is fully congruent with the important principle of 'making the thinking explicit'. So, for instance, in a science lesson you might say to a child, 'Well done Tony, you watched the experiment closely and have come up with two ideas about why the liquids might have changed colour when they were mixed.' Depending on how conversant the children are with the 'vocabulary of thinking' you could add, 'So you've demonstrated your ability to concentrate, shown your observational skills and proved you can do inferential thinking using knowledge you learned earlier.' Since Tony has self-evidently demonstrated good thinking the praise you give must necessarily be sincere.

A further benefit of feeding the thinking back in this way is that it explains to everyone else in the class what Tony has just done, and because all of us like sincere praise other children will be tempted to copy his successful piece of thinking.

Another point to bear in mind when giving praise where it's due is the notion of 'criteria of quality'. In a thinking classroom these will amount to much more than just remembering facts. Broadly speaking the kinds of thinking you feed back to the children are in themselves criteria of quality, which remain valid even if Tony's informed suggestions about why the liquid changed colour prove to be wrong. The fact is that he thought the problem through and it is this you are crediting.

You can use the two important elements of thinking as criteria of quality:

- making fresh connections;
- looking at things in different ways.

These can apply in just about any subject area. So if in that science lesson you want the children to think further about why the liquids changed colour you can prompt them by saying, 'Remember, though, we weren't just mixing the liquids... Yes Sian?' And when Sian tells you that the liquids were also heated you can offer sincere praise for the new connection she's made in her mind.

In creative writing two of the most important criteria of quality as far as I'm concerned are:

- the use of plain, straightforward language that gets the reader's imagination to do plenty of work; and

- the use of a descriptive detail that creates a vivid impression in the reader's mind and which delivers some kind of emotional impact.

A favourite pre-writing workshop of mine is to ask children to look at a black and white picture and, after noticing details, to imagine the picture is in colour (and subsequently to ask them to hear sounds, feel textures etc). So Karl might say, 'Ah, I can see in my mind that the leaves are reddish and yellowish, and they're spinning in the wind…'

This might seem like a fairly run-of-the-mill response, but notice what Karl has achieved. He has:

- turned his attention inward and noticed his own thoughts;
- concentrated on his mental impression long enough to become aware of the colour and movement of the leaves (demonstrating visual and 'kinaesthetic' thinking); and
- had the courage to make his idea public.

In this case I would feed back to Karl what he has done and add, 'So you are not a lazy thinker. I also like the way you helped me to imagine those leaves by giving me two colour words, joining them together and then doing that trick of adding 'ish' to the end. And I really like the little rhyming sounds of "spinning in the wind". Well done.'

This interaction with Karl, which would take less than a minute, turns out to be remarkably rich when it comes to the teaching of thinking – and of creative writing too, since you have let all of the children in the class into Karl's 'linguistic tricks' of using two joined adjectives with their ends modified, and the alliterative technique displayed in 'spinning in the wind'. Whether Karl did these intentionally or not doesn't matter, because the chances are that he and other children will more likely use them deliberately in future.

We'll pick up the idea of criteria of quality elsewhere in the book. In philosophy, for instance, they can be found when children follow the 'etiquette of enquiry' (see **p. 95**). In the field of emotional resourcefulness quality work has been done when a child shows he can control his emotions, especially demonstrating the ability to modify negative ones.

Emergent understanding is another area where praise can be applied. This requires us to look at what a child is doing (nearly) right, rather than just judging it as wrong. So if in his piece of writing Karl puts 'The cats' eyes' sparkled in the moonlight' instead of 'The cat's eyes sparkled in the moonlight' we can recognise his emergent understanding of possessive apostrophes even if he can't apply the idea accurately at the moment. This doesn't mean that the idea shouldn't be explained to him, or that he shouldn't be asked to correct the error; but at the same time I would also praise him for the conciseness of his sentence and that 'sparkled' was an appropriate and well-chosen word.

Catching children doing something right and telling them so is a principle that works well with the 3PPI formula – finding three points of praise for each point that needs improving. The use of *three* points is psychologically powerful. Once might be chance, twice might be coincidence, but when you find three things that a child has done right he is probably convinced you mean it.

CHAPTER 2
Jumpstart thinking and problem solving in literacy

WRITER AS HERO

As children practise noticing and questioning, their ability to spot inaccuracies will improve. I think it is fair to say that a big problem in developing children's literacy skills is an unwillingness sometimes to take the trouble to 'hone' the writing in terms of reaching for the right word or to fully realise the power of punctuation to aid meaning.

In his book *Teaching as Story Telling*, Professor Kieran Egan (1986) advocates the use of narrative structure as an alternative approach to teaching a range of concepts in different subjects. Important elements of the story form are:

- the conflict between hero and villain
- the central problem created by the villain
- the hero's quest in endeavouring to defeat the villain
- the hero's determination and fortitude in the face of difficulties and setbacks
- the whole structure of the story being geared towards a resolution of the problem.

It is impossible in this short section to do justice to the elegance of Egan's ideas, but even just touching on the notion of the 'narrative model' for learning offers several useful insights.

In literacy the 'villain' displays a number of base features that define him as a bad guy. He will:

- try and trick you with a clever use of words
- attempt to persuade you slyly

- try and stir up your emotions for his own ends
- seek to keep you powerless through encouraging apathy.

In other words the villain is portrayed as the way in which others' use of language can manipulate us, but also through the unwillingness of the writer to make an effort to empower himself through the more artful use of words. This second feature is not a negative criticism of the children so much as an opportunity to suggest how they can become the 'hero' and thereby empower themselves.

The noble qualities of the hero as we've seen include determination and fortitude. While I would always advocate making writing as enjoyable as possible, writing well requires a complex set of interconnecting skills that call for hard work to master. Suggesting to children that effort is a heroic quality while their 'learning journey' is the hero's quest might well make a difference in motivating them.

The hero metaphor can be reinforced by pointing out other desirable features of learning to write more skilfully:

- Writing is *making*. A good piece of written work is crafted. As such a craftsman takes pains to do his best and can be justly proud when he succeeds.
- Writing is also 'making public' (which is where the idea of publishing originates). We can craft our thoughts and feelings into words and when this is done well we will have given ourselves a more powerful voice. Furthermore, while thoughts themselves are invisible and fleeting, in written form they serve as a lasting legacy of who we are as individuals.
- A piece of writing doesn't just convey our ideas to others; it is also a record of the decisions and judgements we've made in crafting the work in the way we did – of choosing one word over another or selecting a particular comparison etc. Considering various possibilities, making judgements, reaching conclusions, making decisions – in short trying to get the writing to work – are in themselves noble and desirable qualities.

- A well-crafted piece of writing is aesthetically pleasing, a thing of beauty. This applies to writing of any kind, not just stories and poems.
- The artful use of language through word choice and accurate use of punctuation prevents us from becoming victims. Language is both a strong shield and a sharp sword in the fight against those who would seek to manipulate or confuse us.
- One aspect of the power of writing is that it can create thoughts and feelings in others that they might not otherwise have had. Writing opens the doorway to other worlds of understanding, broadening our experience in diverse and valuable ways.
- The world itself can become a richer and more wonderful place as our ability grows to frame it in language. Becoming 'heroes of language' makes our 'journey' more interesting and helps our other quests in life to succeed.

Help children to appreciate the notion of 'writer as hero' by asking them to create their own coat of arms that illustrates the qualities we've been discussing. You might also suggest designing a villain too, doing his best to defeat us – and failing.

'I CAN'T THINK OF ANYTHING TO WRITE!'

This is a common cry for some children, but a problem that can easily be fixed. Here are various techniques for helping children to generate ideas for stories (we've looked at a couple of them elsewhere):

- *Coin flip game.* This can be a whole-class, group or individual activity. Show the children a picture or just put a sentence on the board, then ask them to come up with yes/no questions that will be answered by the flip of a coin. Extend the game by inviting open questions that the children have to translate into closed ones. So, 'Who lives in that house?' becomes 'Does more than one person live in that house?'

  Any given open question can give rise to more than one closed question, however. Write a suggested open question on the board and collect children's ideas for closed questions that come out of it. Ask children to think about whether they would ask these questions in any particular order, giving reasons for their decisions. Ask them also to choose a question and flip the coin to answer it: does the outcome affect any of the other questions? Which? How?

Something else you can do is guide the children's questioning by suggesting that they ask about character, plot and setting.

- *The Merlin Game.* Use a story the children know and change it in these ways: make bigger, make smaller, take something away, stretch, turn something around, change one thing for another. These parameters are deliberately vague so that they can be interpreted in different ways, so 'make bigger' could mean making a character physically bigger or turning a minor character into a main one, making the story longer, using longer words (see page **25** for more details on the Merlin Game).

- *Link to think.* Ask each child to write or draw an object on a piece of paper. Put all of the pieces in an envelope. Take out two of them and say to the class, 'If you were going to use these in a story, what would the story be about? Tell me in a sentence if you can.' The chances are that quite soon a child will suggest linking three objects, then four… This is all to the good. As children seek to link more and more, allow them more sentences to tell their 'stories in a nutshell'.

  Tip: When thinking of ideas for genre stories, obviously the children will need to choose objects relevant to the given genre. Let's suppose you've chosen science fiction. On the board write some vocabulary you would like them to use – accelerate, asteroid, orbit, planet, satellite etc. – and invite them to build it into their sentences linking two (or more) objects.

- *Stackers.* Write a simple sentence on the board, such as, 'The cat sat on the mat.' Then say, 'But instead of a cat what else could we have?' Stack the children's ideas above the word cat. Then say, 'What else could the cat have done on the mat?' Then ask for words to use instead of on and mat, stacking up the children's suggestions as you did for cat. Now ask the children to try different combinations, pointing out that some will work better than others – 'The cloud relaxed inside the table' doesn't work while 'The giant danced around the rock' could be the basis for a story.

Tip: The Stackers game can also be used as a sentence-building tool. Ask the children what kind of cat it might be and stack adjectives before 'cat'. Ask how the cat was sitting and then stack adverbs, etc. Now put in a phrase such as, 'The cat, who belonged to the Jones family, sat on the mat' and ask for other phrases to stack. In this way you can show children how simple sentences become more complex and introduce the concepts of phrases and clauses.

- *Clues Grid.* Ask the children to come up with a piece of information based on a stimulus sentence you've given them, such as, 'The Jones family live in a large house in the country.' Also specify what kind of story the class will be thinking about, let's say a crime thriller in this case. You will need the children to create 36 clues in total. Make a grid using the clues. You can now ask the children to roll dice to select two or more clues at random and use them as the basis of a plot, or they can simply pick as many clues as they want without using dice. The clues grid is also useful if a child is already writing a story but 'gets stuck'; often a dice roll or two will get the ball rolling again.

- *Colour dice rolls.* Create a grid containing five columns and six rows (though the number of columns can vary). Your five columns might be: emotion, action, adverb, object, place. Assign a different colour to each column, making sure you have coloured dice to match. Ask the class to give you examples to fit into each column, so for emotion you might get: 1 fear, 2 anger, 3 unease, 4 confusion, 5 wonderment, 6 determination. When all the columns have been filled, children roll the coloured dice to choose an emotion, action, adverb, object and place at random. So a child might get confusion, chase, carefully, stone, forest. To begin to link these ideas and give the emergent story some structure, a child might now play the coin flip game or come up with a list of open questions to discuss within a group.

Tip: Any activity that incorporates randomness and chance will aid creative thinking by causing the children to think 'unanticipated thoughts'.

BARE BONES WRITING

Two common problems when children are writing are their tendency to snatch at the first thought coming into their heads and rushing to get the work finished. A further problem is that many children, when asked to plan out their story or whatever, will try to compose the piece at a first attempt and virtually write it out in full (with the result that they are more likely to get bored and frustrated when asked to 'go and write the story now').

'Bare bones writing' is a simple technique that helps to address these issues. Give each child a large sheet of paper and ask him to write down a short list of statements; these might be ones that either you or the child have thought of, or ones created between you. So, for example:

> The boy was walking through the forest.
> It was late afternoon.
> He needed to reach the village.
> He heard a voice calling.
> He went to investigate.
> The light was fading.
> He thought he saw a shadowy figure up ahead.
> He walked deeper among the trees.
> He felt nervous but curious.
> He came to a small house in a clearing.
> He went inside.

If the children are creating these statements for themselves, you can prompt them by asking them where the character was, what time of the day or night it was, what was the character doing, what happens next etc. Note that children don't have to know in any more detail than this what their story will be about.

Make sure the children leave large gaps between the statements. Once they have this skeleton the task is to concentrate on one statement at a time and fill in more details, writing these as *notes* – not the story itself – around the statement they're thinking about. So if a child were concentrating on 'The boy was walking through the forest' he might add a few details about the boy's appearance, how he was feeling, what the forest looked like (including colours, sounds, smells etc.).

The statements don't have to be dealt with in order. It might be that the young writer now has some thoughts about the small house in the clearing, so could jump to that sentence next. Nor do children need to make all their notes on any given statement in one sitting. In fact there's a positive benefit in having children come back to the task after a lapse of time, the next day say; the interim counts as potentially fruitful thinking time, and children might also notice things that evening or coming to school next morning that they can use to add to what's already on the sheet.

Bare bones writing is an example of what I call the 'minimal writing strategy'. This is where tasks require relatively little actual writing but lots of thinking beforehand, and is based on the principle that what matters is quality not quantity. Any technique that satisfies those requirements stands more chance of attracting so-called reluctant writers. Minimal writing tasks combined with techniques that show children how to generate and organise their ideas are usually very motivating.

Tip: Consider using the principle of minimal writing when you ask children to correct or redraft their work. Why not ask them to redraft just one scene or even just one paragraph? And instead of telling them to do all of their corrections, suggest that they review the work and make just one or two changes that you and/or they feel improve the work.

FIXING PROBLEMS

Teaching children to write well is as much a matter of establishing a supportive ethos as it is of helping them to understand the technical aspects of grammar, spelling and punctuation. As a general principle my feeling is that as educators we should motivate children to want to write and teach the technical stuff within the more meaningful context of what they are producing. Teaching rules 'in a vacuum', aided only by exercises out of a textbook, feels like a dry and sterile process to me.

One aspect of the ethos I'm talking about is the way in which we correct children's work and, just as importantly, encourage them to correct it for themselves. Within an educational system that is comparative and competitive it is common for children to feel disillusioned when they think they've 'got it wrong' or are not performing as well as others in the class. Maintaining children's interest in writing and their willingness to write can be encouraged in the following ways:

- The name of the game is 'how many ideas can we have and what use can we make of them?' In other words the process of producing finished pieces of writing is about generating, organising and refining ideas. The initial generation of ideas is similar to the technique of brainstorming, where thoughts are allowed to emerge without judgement or further analysis. Such ideas are the 'raw material' from which more polished writing arises. (Note that this is not the same as snatching at the first thought – mentioned elsewhere in the book – or 'making it up as you go along'. These things tend to happen when children are actually trying to compose the work. The generation of ideas happens at the thinking stage prior to writing.)

  The 'what use can we make of them' part of the process is where ideas are examined more reflectively to see if they 'work'; in other words if they have potential and support the logical consistency of the story. Note that framing things in this way – whether ideas work or not – avoids making value judgements about whether ideas are good or bad, better or worse etc. If a core principle of teaching thinking is to *value* the thinking, then there must be an implicit recognition that all ideas have potential.

- The idea of 'emergent understanding' further supports children's learning by shifting the emphasis towards what they are doing right, rather than just picking them up on what they have done wrong. So if Tony writes, 'Yesterday I wented to my friend's house', although 'wented' is incorrect it does show that Tony has a growing understanding of the past tense. Similarly if he misspells 'separate' and writes 'seperate' he has got seven letters right out of eight, so his understanding of how to spell the word is reasonable. Thinking in this way reminds us that children are still learning and emphasises the value and power of 'yet' – they are not where we want them to be yet.

- The children's author Douglas Hill always spoke about 'fixing problems' when he was writing a book. This idea fits in well with the notion of making a story 'work' as an effective piece of fiction. So in marking and commenting on children's writing we can point out where the problems lie and talk about how we might help a child to fix them. Framing the task of correcting and improving in this way again avoids clumsy and unhelpful value judgements to do with quality.

- *The 3PPI technique.* In marking children's work we can be more elegantly supportive by looking for three points of praise for each area that needs improvement. This exploits the psychological 'power of three', as mentioned on page **49**.

VISUALISE!

Sometimes the quality and richness of children's writing suffer because the children have not noticed their thoughts in enough detail. Turning the attention inward and becoming more aware of what we are thinking, and then manipulating those thoughts, is known as metacognition and is a skill that can be developed in various ways:

- *Picture work.* Show the children a black and white picture. First ask them to notice anything in the picture and to tell you what they've noticed. (This is not a frivolous activity but gives children practice in focusing their attention on small details.) Then ask the children to imagine that the picture is in colour and to tell you what they see. Then focus on sounds. Encourage children to notice various elements of sound: volume, pitch, direction, length, continuous or intermittent etc. Ask them then to 'step into' the picture and become aware of tactile impressions: temperature, weather, textures and so on. The more details that children are able to imagine the more choice they have of what they can put into their writing.

- Develop children's concentration by asking them to visualise in detail a sequence of events such as making a cup of tea or walking around the supermarket as you fill up the trolley.
- Allow children to gain more control over their thoughts by asking them to imagine a simple object such as a tennis ball. Give them a series of instructions for changing the ball in various ways, allowing a pause of ten seconds or so between each instruction – make the ball float, make it larger, turn it purple, turn it inside out etc.
- Get children to pair up. Give them a sentence such as, 'The boy was watching TV at home.' One child in each pair is the visualiser and the other is the questioner. The visualiser begins by telling his partner what he imagines. After this the questioner asks for more details – 'So what is the boy wearing? What does the room look like? Go and look out of the window; what do you see?' After a few minutes the children change roles.
- Take a story extract and ask the children what they are noticing over and above what is mentioned in the text.

For instance, after a class had read this paragraph they came up with the further details that follow it:

Shadowfane Manor is a large Elizabethan house that has gone to ruin now. It lies almost forgotten amidst extensive oakwoods in a corner of rural England. No one thinks of going there, especially the local people who regard the place with dread, although they can never be persuaded to say why. The house shelters no ghosts – at least none that have been discovered – and the atmosphere of peace that surrounds the spot is like nothing you find in any city.

- boarded-up windows/broken windows
- dark rooms, no lights on
- green walls where water has trickled from cracked gutters
- weeds growing close to the house
- ivy growing up the side of the house
- rotten wood (the child was thinking of wooden beams on the outside of the house)
- big tall chimneys made of bricks.

Extend the activity by asking the children to go inside the house and notice even more:

- dark and dusty
- rotten furniture
- wallpaper peeling
- broken floorboards
- mould on the walls in the kitchen
- crumbling carpets
- lots of cobwebs
- mouse droppings.

Running this activity regularly helps children to develop such noticing as a habit and will further enrich the reading experience.

- Sometimes 'failures of visualisation' crop up in stories. Show the children examples of these so that they will be better able to avoid them in their own work:
  - Running into the room, he threw open the window as he switched on the light.
  - Williams saw the chaos in the street below and rubbed his nose, wondering what it would sound like.
  - Like Susanna, John had dark brown hair, with enormous eyebrows, a fine moustache and handsome beard.
  - Her eyes twinkled, fluttered, met his, dropped to the floor, then went back to the jewels. He picked them up, held them for a moment then returned them to her with a smile.

SLIDING SCALE

Give the class a series of clues that suggest a scenario. For instance:

The TV in the lounge is on standby.
A bath is being filled upstairs.
The front door is open.
There are wet footprints on the stairs.
A police siren can be heard in the distance.

Two people are hurrying down the street.

- First of all ask children to suggest what might be happening, using as many of the clues as possible. So, for instance, there might have been an accident farther up the road. The police are racing to the scene. The person filling the bath heard the accident and has rushed out to see what's happened.
- Draw a line on the board and number along it 1–6. The scenario above would be 1 on the scale as it is the kind of thing that could easily happen. If the police were racing towards a flying saucer that had landed in the park, that would be 6 on the scale. Ask the children to decide where along the line they would place the scenarios they came up with.
- Now ask the children to come up with further example scenarios using as many of the clues as possible. Begin at 1 and collect ideas as you progressively move along the scale towards 6.
- Now deliberately introduce the idea of genre. Ask for scenarios that lie at a particular point along the scale and are of a chosen genre. So you might want a romance that's two on the scale, or a crime thriller that's four etc. (bearing in mind that fantasy, science fiction and horror are by their very nature tending towards the higher numbers).
- Ask each child in the class to think of another clue that is 'genre neutral', i.e. that doesn't of itself change the collection of clues into fantasy or science fiction scenarios. Add one clue to the list. What further scenarios can the children now think of? Add other clues one by one to increase the challenge of the task.

The point of the sliding scale is to dampen the tendency that some children have to 'let their imaginations run away with them'. Some boys in particular automatically use the weirdest and wackiest ideas they can think of, rather than choosing ideas that build towards a believable and logically consistent story.

ARE YOU PERSUADED?

Raising children's awareness of persuasive language is an important area of developing literacy and thinking skills. Show the following sentences and ask the children to suggest how they are trying to influence our thinking:

> More than 1,900 people flocked to the concert.
> Less than 2,000 people bothered to turn up at the concert.
> (Controlling the way the reader looks at the subject)

> Wouldn't you like to live in a country where people are happier, healthier and more contented?
> Don't you think it's reasonable to want to earn a good living?
> Do you ever feel that society's problems aren't being dealt with properly?
> (Using questions that the reader can easily agree with)

> It was a mouth-watering meal.
> The joke was hilarious.
> John felt terrified.
> It was a perfect evening.
> Ann replied furiously.
> (Using strong action adjectives/verbs/adverbs)

> Can you imagine being happy, wealthy and successful?
> Just pretend for a moment that you've already got everything you ever wanted. What does that feel like right now?
> Suppose you bought our product. Just picture how many ways that will make your life better!
> (Appealing to the imagination)

Sometimes the way a statement is 'designed' is intended to influence our point of view. Ask the children if they can spot the persuasive features in the following sentence:

> Now the government is making it **even HARDER** for you to buy your own home!!

They may come up with some or all of the following:

- 'Now' suggests that the government has previously done other things to make life harder for us;

- use of bold text for emphasis;
- use of capitals to suggest strength of feeling (similar to the way in which ongoing use of capitals in emails is taken to be 'shouting');
- the phrase 'even harder' suggests that the government had already made it hard to buy a home;
- use of second person pronoun 'you' speaks directly to the reader;
- choice of 'home' rather than house or property to further personalise the message;
- double exclamation marks to reinforce strength of feeling.

As a greater challenge, ask the children to notice the differences between the following statements, both in terms of visual differences and the way they are trying to influence us:

Knowing your times tables by heart is very useful.
Knowing your times tables by heart can often be very useful.
Knowing your times tables by heart up to twelve-times can often be very useful.
Knowing your times tables by heart is always very useful.
Most people would agree that knowing your times tables by heart is often very useful.
Clearly, knowing your times tables by heart is always very useful.
Clearly, without a doubt, knowing your times tables by heart is always very useful.

METAWRITING

Essentially this is writing about writing, where children are encouraged to comment on the writing process itself as well as adding any further ideas to their story or essay (this avoids what some children feel to be the tedium of redrafting). Get the children to rule a vertical line down the centre of the page: the piece of work is written in one column and the annotations written subsequently in the other. Sometimes it is best for children to annotate their work soon after writing it, when it is fresh in their mind. However, when children look at work they did months before they often write more comments, partly because their literacy has improved in the interim.

Another version of annotated writing is where a story appears in one column while questions and 'mini tasks' that you have written go in the other, with enough space between for the children's responses (see Figure 2.1). The story or whatever doesn't have to be the children's own work of course: it's much more economical for you time-wise to use the same story for every child.

Stickers, questions/instructions and child's ideas go here:	Story, poem, letter etc goes here.
  What is the amulet made of? Who is the true owner? How can you use it at the start of the story? It's made of gold and different precious stones. The true owner is the centaur. It was given to him by the god of the mountain years ago. It has been stolen by two of the King's guards [Note: you can ask questions in stages as the child finishes each part of the story. Based on what has been written, further questions might be…] How did the guards know about the amulet? How might Kefro go about getting it back? Who could he ask to help him? How might you use this picture in the next part of your story…? 	Once long ago in the land beyond the Misty Sea a centaur woke from his long winter sleep. All centaurs hibernate in caves where they are sheltered from the freezing fog that rolls in from the ocean. The centaur who woke – his name was Kefro – opened his eyes, blinked and stretched. He was in the middle of a lovely big yawn when, to his horror, he realised that his precious amulet had been stolen. It had been given to him when he was very young by the god of the mountain, as a token of respect to Kefro's father, who had died helping the mountain god to protect the high peaks from invasion. The amulet was made of gold with precious jewels – emeralds, amethysts, sapphires and sunstones – decorating it. It was worth a lot of money, but more important than that was that Kefro loved the amulet. Besides, if he could not find it he would be dishonouring his friend the mountain god.

Figure 2.1 Metawriting

Tip: To create the 'stickers' referred to in Figure 2.1, use the 'envelopes and labels' tool in your word processing program. Import pictures into the cells and print them off on a sheet of stickers. You can use coloured images, though many children enjoy colouring them in for themselves. Picture stickers allow children to illustrate their stories quickly and easily, and brighten up your/the children's annotations.

ASSESSING WRITING

The primary reason for teaching thinking skills is to help children to become more independent thinkers, both creatively and critically. Showing them ways of forming judgements about writing – their own and others', fiction and non-fiction – is thus an important part of the process.

We have already talked about establishing an 'ethos for thinking' where the children's ideas are valued, where effort is appreciated and where the distinction is made between attainment and achievement (see Introduction). When such an environment is in place most children tend to offer their opinions more readily.

Ask children first to look at the overall purpose and intended audience of the writing. Is it to inform, persuade, entertain, teach you how to do something, give an overview (e.g. an encyclopaedia article)? Who is the book mainly written for – children, adults, beginners, experts?

In assessing fiction guide the children to consider the following:

- How much did you enjoy the story (on a 1–6 scale where 6 means 'enjoyed very much')?
- Were there any parts that were especially interesting, dramatic etc? How did the writer achieve that?
- Are there any phrases or sentences that you found particularly impressive? Make a note of a couple of them.
- Were there any parts of the story that you thought didn't work so well? Give your reasons for this.

- What emotional impact did the story have on you – did it make you laugh, feel sad, get scared etc.? If you haven't already done so, mention how you think the author achieved that.
- Write a short review of the book (a paragraph) recommending or not recommending the book to other readers.

In assessing the information content of non-fiction, suggest to the children that they look out for the following:

- *Organisation and content.* Do the contents of the book seem to be laid out in a useful way? Glancing at the table of contents, does the book seem to contain the information you're looking for?
- *Date of publication.* In some subjects, like science, information can become out of date quickly. How recently was the book published? Will the information you're looking for date quickly, slowly or not at all?
- *Author.* What information is given about the author? Is he or she an expert in the field? What else has the author written?
- *Bibliography and references.* Has the author referred to the work of other writers? How important or useful is that for the information you're looking for?
- *Illustrations.* Are there illustrations and diagrams in the book and if so how clear and helpful did you find them?
- *Coverage.* Did the book cover the topic well enough to supply you with all the information you needed?

Tip: Finally, when children are working with facts suggest that they look at two or more sources for the information, noting any discrepancies or differences of opinion.

CHAPTER 3
Jumpstart thinking and problem solving in science

OBSERVATION GAMES

Sharpen children's observational skills by giving them things to notice, but also helping them to devise their own observation challenges.

- Have a tray of objects in the classroom. Change something about the tray each day – add, take away or substitute an object or change their configuration. Begin by making the changes obvious but gradually make them increasingly difficult to spot.
- *Observation Journal.* Supply each child with a book where they can write about and draw things they notice. These can be brief character descriptions of people they see, interesting objects they come across, events and incidents etc. Give the children particular objects to study closely and then describe, such as leaves, stones, shells or pieces of wood. Ask children to get into small groups and give each group two similar objects, say two leaves. Get the groups to discuss similarities and differences between their objects.

Observation challenges can be brief, as above, or long-term. Changes in the weather, the phases of the moon or the way a tree changes through the seasons are all suitable topics.

Extend the activity by asking children to compare scientific and literary/poetical descriptions of the same object. How does the language of an astronomy book talking about the moon for instance differ from references to the moon in poetry? (Type 'famous poems about the moon' into a search engine to get plenty of examples.)

SPOTTING PATTERNS

Scientific progress relies heavily on people's ability to notice patterns and cycles in nature. Jumpstart your children's pattern recognition skills by trying these easily organised activities:

- Draw dots on a sheet of paper and give copies to each child or working group. Ask the children to see if they can join some of them to make recognisable objects, animals and shapes.
- Show the class star maps. Maps showing the unlabelled shapes of the constellations are readily available online. Ask the children to discuss what different constellations are meant to be. Can the children join the stars in other ways to make different star patterns?

  Literacy link: Tell the children some of the myths and legends attached to some of the constellations. There is also benefit in looking at the origins of star names and the names of other celestial objects.
- *Counter tray.* Create different sequences and patterns of coloured counters on a tray and invite children to work out what they represent. For example, five blue coins and two red ones mean the five weekdays plus Saturday and Sunday. Three green, three red, three yellow and three blue represent the twelve months and four seasons of the year. Ask children to think of sequences of their own – in one class Alison asked if she could have control of the counter tray for that whole week. On Monday the other children counted twelve purple coins and sixteen green ones; Tuesday, fourteen purple and sixteen green, the numbers varying slightly each day. No one spotted the pattern: purple counters represented the boys in the class who were present and green counters stood for the girls.

CATEGORIES OF QUESTIONS

The distinction between open and closed questions is a basic one that all children need to know. Here are some other ideas for getting children to think about questions:

- *Question Hunt.* Ask the children to find at least one question from each of these categories:
  a) A question with an answer that is always right for everybody.
  b) A question with an answer that is always right for one person and never right for another (for example, 'What is your address?').
  c) A question with at least one right answer that is different now from what it used to be (for example, 'Pluto used to be called a planet but now it's a dwarf planet').
  d) A couple of questions where different people's opinions can be counted as 'right' answers.
  e) A question that nobody really knows the answer to.
  f) A question that makes you and your friends want to ask lots of other questions (for example, 'Is it better to be alive now than it was a hundred years ago?')
- Ask the class to suggest what categories these questions could be put into. Note that some questions could fit into more than one category. Having discussed and decided upon the most suitable or useful categories, ask the class to come up with further questions to put into them. For example:
  1 What is 4 + 3?
  2 What is the capital city of America?
  3 Do you like milk?
  4 Are you tall?
  5 What is blue?
  6 What is your favourite story?
  7 How far away are the stars?
  8 Why do we have best friends?
  9 How can we find true happiness?

  Tip: You'll notice that some of these questions are deliberately ambiguous. All credit to any child who responds with another question, as in, 'Do you mean what is the colour blue *itself* or an example of something that is blue?' Seeking clarification of questions is an important skill in all of the areas we explore in this book.
- *Here's the question, what are the answers.* Give the children a word or sentence that counts as an answer and ask them to think of as many questions as possible that have that answer. For example:

the answer is three, what are the questions? The answer is London, what are the questions?

- Occasionally ask children what they think is the most useful and/or interesting question they've asked today and why they think that.

ASSUMPTIONS

An assumption is a conclusion we reach or a judgement we make in the absence of any substantial evidence. Here are some activities to help children to think about when they are making assumptions:

- Here are the clues from the sliding scale game on page **60**:

  The TV in the lounge is on standby.
  A bath is being filled upstairs.
  The front door is open.
  There are wet footprints on the stairs.
  A police siren can be heard in the distance.
  Two people are hurrying down the street.

- Ask the children to indicate if they agree with the following statements:
  a) Someone has been watching the TV recently.
  b) There is somebody upstairs.
  c) The person had just stepped into the bath but then heard the police siren and came rushing out to see what was going on.
  d) The two hurrying people know each other.
  e) The two people are hurrying in the direction of the police siren.

- The fact is that we don't actually *know* if any of the above statements are true. The TV could have been on standby since yesterday; someone might have turned on the bath taps and then come downstairs; and so on. Whether children indicated yes or no to the statements, they were reacting to what they *thought they knew*; in other words they were making an assumption.

- Ask the children to imagine they are detectives. Give them the following scenario and then invite questions, which you are to answer yes or no to as far as possible.

  Imagine a locked room. Opposite the door are a pair of French windows. They are open but heavy drapes have been pulled across. It's stormy weather outside. Near the drapes there is a small table. On the floor near the table there is smashed glass. On the carpet around the glass there is some liquid. In the room Janet and John lie dead. What's happened?

- Of course you'll need the answer to be able to answer the children's questions – it's on page **132**. Before looking, decide for yourself what you think has gone on...

  Now that you know the answer, keep the children guessing for a few minutes (they can get very frustrated if you spin it out longer than this!)

  Extend the game by inviting the children to come up with other scenarios that tempt their classmates to make assumptions.

  (Another good one is the story about a man and his son who had an accident when rock climbing. The man was killed but the boy lived. He was rushed to hospital but the head surgeon who first saw him gasped, 'Oh no, that's my son!' How can this be? Answer: If you assumed that the surgeon was a man, you might puzzle over this story for ages.)

- The assumptions we've been looking at so far are false assumptions – in other words we jump to the wrong conclusions by misinterpreting the evidence. There are however many so-called 'common sense assumptions' we make based on our own experience and/or because we've been told that they are so. We rely on common sense assumptions to make life easier or more readily understandable. Here are a few to ponder over:
  1 Soon after the traffic lights turn red the green man appears.
  2 The sun will rise tomorrow.
  3 I've seen thousands of black crows in my life but never a white one, so all crows must be black.
  4 Water boils at 100°C.
  5 I'm five miles away from Jim, my appointment with him is due to start in one minute. I'm late!

- Again you might quiz the children by asking them how they actually *know* that these examples are so. You can be duly impressed if any child replies:
  1 Unless there is an electrical fault.
  2 It's not the sun that's moving, it's the Earth.
  3 We cannot say this is absolutely true because white crows might actually exist, we just haven't seen one yet (this is the famous 'one white crow' dictum in science).
  4 At sea level on Earth, but not at the top of Everest, on the Moon etc.
  5 I haven't missed my appointment yet: I have another minute to go. Anyway, I'm using Skype to meet with Jim.
- Ask the children to give you some of the common sense assumptions they make to make life easier.

BIAS

Bias is the use of various tricks of language to try and influence our opinion, usually to agree with that of the writer. Here are some common techniques used to bias an argument:

exaggeration and/or understatement
emotive words
generalizations
selection of particular examples to support a general outlook
'weighting' or distortion of 'facts'
opinion disguised as truth
use of rhetorical questions (often beginning obviously/ surely/clearly etc.)
lack of or inadequate evidence to support an assertion
lack of or inadequate reasoned argument or judgement
creating false links between two or more ideas, opinions, arguments etc.

- Show the following letter to the children and ask them how Albert Hall is trying to make you see his point of view (and agree with it).

Global Warming Is Not My Problem!

Sir – Following your article last week on how 'Mankind is responsible for the world heating up', I strongly object to being tarred with the same brush as people who treat their environment like a dustbin! I am always extremely careful to recycle my rubbish and hate to see uncaring slobs dropping litter on the pavement. Surely it's not too much trouble for them to put their trash where it belongs, in the bin? We are bombarded with stuff on the TV and in the newspapers about keeping our streets tidy and treating our world with respect – don't the eco-vandals who drop litter watch TV? Or is it that they just can't read?

Anyone in their right mind can see that the climate is out of control. More and more experts are telling us that unless we mend our ways now our beautiful Earth is doomed. Clearly we don't want our children to inherit a wilderness. So instead of blaming people like me – people who always try their very best to protect the environment – we should be coming down like a ton of bricks on the ones who really are behind global warming – the drivers of big cars, the thoughtless people who fly off on luxury holidays three times a year, the two-car families, the ones who leave all their electrical equipment on standby... The list is endless.

So use your newspaper to get these people to change their minds, and stop blaming me for the catastrophe that's just around the corner!

Yours faithfully, Albert Hall, Plumstead

- Choose some appropriate headlines to show the children (a few headlines covering the same story is useful). Ask the children, 'Do the different newspapers try and make you react in different ways?' 'What tricks do they use?'
- Bias is a kind of persuasion. Ask children to look at some adverts on TV and in magazines to try and spot some techniques of persuasion.

SCIENTIFIC LANGUAGE IN ADVERTISING

'Science' is often used to try and sell us things, appealing to the authority of scientists to give us 'facts' about the products on offer. Being an independent thinker means not necessarily taking what we are told at face value but (time and inclination permitting) looking a little deeper.

One interesting aspect of the scientific gloss found in some advertising is the way impressive sounding scientific terms are used as a persuasive technique. Looking at the language is a useful opportunity to develop children's questioning and reasoning skills:

- Show the class an appropriate selection of adverts from TV and magazines. Ask the children to pick out words and phrases that sound scientific – examples include clinically proven, specially formulated, advanced technology, now even better, scientific tests prove that…, 95% (e.g.) of the people we asked, up to 100% effective, new improved, premium quality, the facts show that…, organic, natural, it's what doctors/dentists/scientists recommend, new data that may completely change your mind. Also look out for ultra, anti, mega, multi, etc.
- Take some of these phrases and compile a list of open questions about them. What does 'clinically' mean? What scientific tests prove that…? etc. (You may not have the opportunity to look for the answers, but the point of the task is to raise children's awareness of persuasive language.)
- Check the meanings of words such as ultra and multi. Why might they be used instead of 'beyond' and 'many'?
- Check a range of adverts to see if scientific-sounding terms are used more for certain kinds of products.
- Ask children to notice how science and scientists are portrayed more generally in advertising (laboratory setting, white lab coats etc.).
- Split the class into groups and ask each to design an advert for a product. This could include a new scientific name for the item plus a short description using some of the terms the children have already looked at.

Tip: These tasks can act as a precursor to a wider study of 'pseudo science' and how and if 'science' as a human endeavour can answer all possible questions. Thinking about this in itself is a useful lead-in to philosophical enquiry.

CAUSES AND CORRELATIONS

An important aspect of scientific thinking is to make the distinction between a cause and a correlation (which is where things are associated but one thing doesn't give rise to another). Here are some activities to help children to think about this distinction:

- Ask the class to come up with some everyday examples of one thing causing another. For example, 'I turn on the tap and water comes out', 'I switch on the kettle and the water soon boils', 'I knock the cup and my tea spills.'
- Ask the children to look for the faulty reasoning behind 'false correlations' such as:
  a) As the forest fire spread more firemen were visible, therefore an increase in the number of firemen caused the fire to spread. However, is it true to say that the spreading fire caused more firemen to appear?
  b) More ice cream is sold in summer than in winter. More people drown in the summer than during any other season, thus eating more ice cream causes more people to drown.
  c) Carbon dioxide levels in the atmosphere have been increasing along with obesity in the population, so carbon dioxide must cause people to eat more and become fatter.
  Tip: Make children aware of 'reasoning' words such as therefore, thus, so, because, must etc. Their use doesn't mean a correlation is 'real'.
- Invite the children to think up further false correlations, if possible using phenomena that (as far as we know) are real, such as the fact that carbon dioxide levels are rising and the problem of obesity is becoming more acute.

DEFINING AND CLASSIFYING

Science has been called a 'GAS process' (Go And See), whereas philosophy is more properly a 'SATT process' (Sit And Think/ Talk). However, both aim to achieve a 'shared clarity of meaning', which is aided greatly by the skills of defining and classifying. Help children to practise these skills in the following ways:

- Practise *attributing* (listing characteristics) as a first step towards defining things. Ask the children to write the word 'cat', for example, in the middle of a large sheet of paper and then to write the characteristics of a cat around it.
- Test some of the attributes the children have listed. Most groups will say that a cat has fur. If a furless cat was bred would it still be a cat? What if a furless cat was found naturally in the wild – could we still call it a cat? What if biologists bred a cat that barked like a dog – would it still be as much a cat as one that meowed?
- Show how defining and classifying are linked. If a cat is an animal, how could we define 'animal'? After the children have discussed this, show them how cats fit into the larger classification of animals.
- As a precursor towards more philosophical thinking, challenge the class by asking: 'Do we agree that one of the characteristics of a cat is that it is alive?' (hopefully yes). 'Since we do not completely understand what "life" is, is it true to say that we cannot *completely* define what a cat is?'
- Take the challenge further by trying to define concepts such as justice, love, truth etc. It is not important for the children to be doing 'proper' philosophical enquiry at this stage; by listening carefully to others, giving examples (and counter examples), asking questions and restating ideas, they are already practising the skills needed for more formalised and sophisticated P4C.
- Ask the children to look around the room and write down the names of things that could be put into larger groups because of their shared characteristics. Are there any objects that fit into more than one group (e.g. ruler – plastic and measuring device)?

COMMON SENSE

Albert Einsten said that common sense is what tells us the Earth is flat. This reinforces the 'Go And See' process that characterises true science. While science is based on our direct experience of the world, its success lies in not taking the world at face value but by questioning, measuring, experimenting – in short collecting data to help create, support and verify theories about how we think the natural world works.

Help children to understand both the everyday value but also the limitations of common sense with the following activities:

- Discuss what we might mean by 'common sense'. Make a list of common examples of people using their common sense – looking carefully before crossing the road, not dipping your finger in a saucepan of water to check that it's coming to the boil etc.
- Look at some well-known proverbs and assess how far the advice they give counts as common sense:

    A bad beginning makes a good ending.
    A fool and his money are soon parted.
    A miss is as good as a mile.
    A wise man changes his mind sometimes, a fool never.
    Delays are dangerous.
    Flattery brings friends, truth enemies.

    Tip: This is a good opportunity to point out the figurative nature of many proverbs such as, 'A bird in the hand is worth two in the bush.'
- Greater understanding of natural patterns, cycles and laws allows science to make predictions about the likelihood of phenomena happening in the future. Introduce this notion by playing some prediction games with the children, asking them to work out missing letters and numbers from sequences you've given them.
- Contrast scientific predictions (such as weather forecasting) with non-scientific predictions such as those found in newspaper

astrology columns. Discuss with the children whether statements like the following are 'predictive' and if so, in what way?

Partnerships are likely.
You are on a threshold.
Your plans will bring rewards.
Important messages are due.

- Some of the things that science has discovered are *counterintuitive*; that is, they are contrary to common sense. As Einstein pointed out, the evidence of our senses seems to tell us that the Earth is flat and unmoving. An internet search will bring up further examples (like water vapour being lighter than air). There are also many optical illusions online that show how easily our minds can be tricked.

INFOSCRAPS

Infoscraps are simply scraps of paper with pieces of information written on them. The technique is very versatile and can be used across a wide age and ability range. Sets of infoscraps are scrambled and the children's task is to put them in the sequence or pattern you've asked for. Here are some ideas you might want to try:

- alphabetical order
- number sequences
  Tip: Include some blank scraps that are still part of the sequence. The children must decide what numbers or letters must go on the blanks to complete the sequence.
- height order of children in the class
- hair length (using diamond ranking, see below)
- eye colour (you can use this idea to introduce Venn Diagrams)
- favourite TV programme (or book, food, drink etc.)
- friendship groups (Venn Diagrams again, or relationship webs).

Not all sets of infoscraps need to be in a linear sequence. The diamond ranking technique allows pieces of information that are equal or equivalent in some way to be placed side by side. The technique is so called because there can be one scrap at the top, then two side by side below that, then three or four side by side below that, tapering back to one scrap at the bottom, thus making a diamond shape. However, the technique doesn't need to be used so rigidly; any number of scraps can be placed side by side. Here are some more infoscrap ideas:

- Create infoscraps with drawings of animals. Ask the children to arrange the animals in various ways – according to size, grouped by Class, Order, Family etc., in order of 'usefulness' to people, in order of rarity (opportunity for research), in order of how much a child or group thought they knew about the animals, in order of how much the animals are wanted as a pet etc.
- Arrange infoscraps with the names of English counties, US States and countries of the world so that their physical proximity reflects to some extent their actual geographical relationship.
- Arrange infoscraps of famous discoveries, inventions and names of scientists in a historical timeline.
- Create sets of infoscraps from a short story that you have read with the children. This might be the complete tale (if very short) or key scenes, fragments of dialogue etc. Groups must recreate the order of events from memory.
- Use infoscraps as a planning tool for argumentative essays. Scraps can be arranged as: for and against, opinion vs fact, chains of reasoning or 'strength' of reasons. Again the diamond ranking tool will prove useful.

HOW RELEVANT?

Make up a set of clues like the ones we looked at in the Sliding Scale idea in Chapter 2 (p. **60**). Ask children first to come up with a believable scenario about what might have happened (i.e. 1–2 on the scale) using as many of the clues as possible. Here is an example:

Clues

A flowerpot beside the west-facing front door of Bedside Manor, a stately home, is on its side.

There are footprints in the flowerbed outside the drawing room window.

There are scratches on the lock to the back door.

The sun is shining.

The exterior windowsills on the north and west sides of the house are wet.

Sets of two holes side by side can be seen occasionally in the grass close to the house.

Two valuable paintings are missing from the drawing room.

One of the garages near the house has no car in it.

There are damp muddy marks in the hallway.

A bronze sculpture of a red heron sits on the drawing room mantelpiece.

The dirty dishes from breakfast are still in the sink in the kitchen.

Scenario

A burglar was sneaking around Bedside Manor looking for a way to get in, having spotted the precious paintings through the drawing room window (leaving his footprints in the flowerbed). He tried to pick the back door lock unsuccessfully. Then he had an idea and looked under the flowerpot by the front door, where he found a key. He got in and stole the paintings. The sets of marks in the grass are impressions left by the window cleaner's ladder. He was at the house earlier. Some windowsills are still wet from his cleaning; they are on the sides of the house out of the sun.

Discuss what 'relevant' means with the class:

- Supposing that story was true, ask the children now to rank the clues in order of relevance, using a 1–6 scale and/or the diamond ranking technique (see the infoscraps idea above).
- Ask the children to invent further relevant clues to support the sneaky burglar story.
- Challenge the children with questions such as:
  a) Why didn't the thief bother to put the overturned flowerpot back upright again? (Another caller at the house might think an overturned pot looks suspicious.)

b) Why did the thief take the two paintings when there were other valuable items that were smaller in the drawing room?

c) How do we know that the window cleaner called before the robbery?

d) How do we know the thief entered the house shortly after the windows were cleaned?

- Now ask the class for further clues that 'blur the issue' and point the finger of blame at someone else, let's say the window cleaner.
- Take one of the irrelevant clues, e.g. the dirty dishes in the sink, and tell the children that this is highly relevant to what happened. Ask them to modify the story and incorporate the now relevant clue. The sneaky guy, the window cleaner or someone else can now be the burglar.

HYPOTHESISING AND INFERRING

Build on the work the children have done in 'How Relevant?' by giving them practice in making inferences to support a hypothesis. (A hypothesis is a supposition based on reasoning without an assumption of its truth. It is more robust than a pure speculation and not as fully tested or verified as a theory. An inference is a conclusion that has been reasoned out by examining the evidence.)

Here are some pieces of evidence about lights that were seen in the sky above the city of Kenniston. Split the class into groups and ask each group to decide what might have caused it, including a timeline in their answer. If they come up with more than one hypothesis ask them to place these in order of 'strength' based on the supporting evidence.

Tip: Use the infoscrap technique to help children work through the evidence. Physically moving the pieces of information around helps children to organise their thoughts and produces a great deal of useful group discussion.

1   The moon rises at 15.37 on 5 September.
2   UFO means 'Unidentified Flying Object'.

3 Just like the sun, the planets and stars set in the west or north-west.

4 The planet Saturn rises in the east at 19.56.

5 A bright meteor streaks across the sky at about ten minutes to nine.

6 At 20.40 Venus is 30° above the horizon.

7 A burned patch is spotted next day by Ben's dad as he travels to work on the Harrowby Road.

8 A small fire was reported to have 'started mysteriously' among some rubbish bags in an alley just north-west of Mr Lee's store.

9 Police are called to Mr Lee's store at 21.35 when the burglar alarm goes off. A break-in has occurred and a cash register has been forced open.

10 On 6 September the local radio reports sightings of four 'strange dark figures' running across West Park at around 21.45 in a north-westerly direction.

11 At 23.00 unexplained flickering lights are seen in Patchley Woods, three miles north-west of Kenniston.

12 On 6 September, midday reports on the local news channel state that four men have been apprehended by police on the coast road near the West Cliff lighthouse.

13 At 21.20 you drive with your older brother along the Clayton Road to pick up a takeaway. The UFOs seem to keep pace with the car.

14 The UFOs seem to be moving in a north-westerly direction.

15 Your friend Gina says that at her parents' barbecue last weekend they launched some lovely sky lanterns. You could see them for miles.

16 There is a motor accident on the Harrowby Road at 20.29. Police and an ambulance arrive on the scene less than ten minutes later.

17 A haystack fire breaks out at East Fields Farm at 18.27. Flames soar sixty feet into the air.

18 On 5 September the local paper, the Kenniston Gazette, reports that Mr Lee spent £20,000 on fireworks for his special late night shopping event.

19 Two miles away to the north-west stands the West Cliff lighthouse.

20 You see the fireworks display at Mr Lee's store as you walk by.

21 By 21.30 the UFOs are very low down in the north-west.

22 Your friend Ben says the flying saucers are probably from Mars.

23 At 21.00 two glowing patches are visible through high cloud on either side of the moon.

24 Your friend Tony says he saw the same UFOs last night at a similar time.

25 It is quite possible intelligent life exists elsewhere in the Universe.

26 There is a disco going on at Kenniston High School.

27 You turn right on to the High Street at 20.37.

28 The UFOs do not change position in relation to one another.

29 One UFO is brighter than the other.

30 The UFOs look like two very bright lights moving slowly along in the west.

31 The rock concert lasers whirl quickly and change colour regularly.

32 You and your friends come out of the cinema and walk east along Auriga Street.

33 There's a rock concert with a laser show going on in West Park.

34 The two UFOs seem to keep the same distance from one another.

35 Venus and Jupiter are in close conjunction this evening.

36 There is a military air base fifteen miles away in Southness.

37 The waxing moon is one quarter full.

38 You see the strange lights at 20.52 to the west.

39 There are some low clouds in the sky, drifting gently in the south-easterly wind.

40 The film finishes at 20.30.

41 Mr Lee's Department Store is hosting a special late-night shopping event, finishing at 21.00.

42 Sunset occurs at 19.37 on 5 September, the day of the sighting.

CHAPTER 4

Jumpstart thinking and problem solving in philosophy

HOW DO YOU EAT AN ELEPHANT?

A little bit at a time. So too in philosophy for children (P4C), building the skills necessary to enjoy a rich and fruitful enquiry is a step by step process. Some of the skills have already been touched on, while the main purpose of the entire book is to encourage the creative and critical kinds of thinking that lie at the heart of philosophical enquiry.

Make explicit the skills that you want children to learn. Create a colourful display, perhaps featuring children's drawings of such skills 'in action'. Give each child a skills checklist and suggest that they monitor themselves and keep a tally of how and when the skills are displayed. Some that you and the children can look out for include:

- really listening (listening with full attention, with respect, without interrupting)
- expressing ideas and views succinctly
- choosing words carefully
- keeping to the point
- saying, 'I want more time to think about that'
- feeling it's OK to change your mind
- including others in the discussion
- agreeing and disagreeing (supported by strong reasons)
- questioning what others say
- restating an idea to check that you've understood it
- giving examples to illustrate a point/offering counter-examples
- answering a point with a question
- building on the ideas and opinions of others

- looking at things from another viewpoint (not necessarily one you agree with).

THE FORTUNATELY-UNFORTUNATELY GAME

This quickfire activity helps children to flip mentally between two viewpoints. Start with a sentence such as: 'Bowman decided to spend a night at home watching TV, but unfortunately...' Invite the children to complete the sentence and use the first idea you hear, for example:

'Unfortunately the TV was broken.'

Then you say something like, 'Unfortunately Bowman's TV was broken. But fortunately...'

A child might say, 'He had a spare in the bedroom.'

Then you would say, 'He had a spare TV in the bedroom. Unfortunately, however...'

And so the game proceeds until the 'story' reaches a natural conclusion or ideas dry up. Alternatively you can specify a time limit – five minutes is reasonable. Apart from giving children experience of flipping between viewpoints, the activity brings the following benefits:

- the unfolding stories are often very amusing and most children will readily play the game whenever you suggest it;
- the game is inclusive. Even those children who do not offer ideas are actively listening to the way the story is going;
- the activity develops children's ability to concentrate. Interest is sustained because of the random factor of not knowing how the story will develop;
- the game can be used to jumpstart ideas during the early stages of planning a story.

The fortunately-unfortunately game can also lead towards an activity called 'flipping the coin', which can help children become more emotionally resourceful.

Some people tend to think negatively almost by default, and sometimes without really noticing. Such a constant stream of negative thoughts might well eventually 'harden' into an attitude that is difficult to shift. However, as soon as a child who engages in negative self-talk *notices* that's what is happening he can take action by immediately thinking a positive opposite. So, '(Unfortunately) I got a low mark for my last piece of work… But (fortunately) I know how I can do better next time.' Or '(Unfortunately) my best friend isn't talking to me… But (fortunately) these phases don't last very long.'

Deliberately thinking positive opposites neutralises the corrosive effect of negative thinking and can with practice turn into the 'fortunately-fortunately' game where the individual concentrates solely on positive outcomes.

Tip: You can find further ideas for using the fortunately-unfortunately game in my book *Jumpstart!Creativity* (2007).

THE IF-THEN GAME

This activity explores causes, effects and consequences. It is linked to the What-If game (Chapter 1, p. **35**), which in fact can be used as a source of ideas for trying out if-then.

The game takes the form of a 'chain' of linked ideas. So, using the notion we met earlier – 'What if people grew normally until they were 30 and then started to shrink, so that by age 60 you were only six inches tall?' (Chapter 1, p. **36**) – we get something like:

1   If people shrank steadily through their adult life then older people would become more and more vulnerable.
2   If older people became more vulnerable then ones that were evil would not be so able to do bad things.

3   If some older people still wanted to do bad things they could pay younger, bigger people to do them.

4   If younger people wanted to do bad things they could go ahead anyway. Also they could blackmail older people into giving up more of their money.
    Teacher: OK, let's go back to the starting point about older people shrinking. What might be another consequence of that happening?

5   If older people kept shrinking then we would need to invent new kinds of machines to help them – like tiny vehicles for them to travel in.

6   If we did invent tiny vehicles they would need special, separate roads because using our ordinary roads would be too dangerous.

7   If tiny people needed separate roads then to be really safe they'd need special communities just for themselves.

8   If they lived in separate communities then it would be much more difficult to look after them if they became ill.

9   Although if they lived among younger, bigger people then you could adapt houses so that smaller people could be safe and with their children...

As we have seen, it is quite in order to guide the discussion if a chain of ideas fizzles out. Taking the talk back to the original point is good training for children anyway. Notice too how even a fantastical scenario can lead to consideration of real-world issues like making provision for older people or people who fall ill; the structure of communities; and how technology can contribute to the kinds of lives we want to lead.

PLAYING WITH SYLLOGISMS

A syllogism is a logical argument made up of three parts: a major idea (or premise), a minor idea and a conclusion that comes out of those ideas. In looking at this pattern of reasoning we need to see if the premises themselves are true without exception and whether the reasoning of the argument itself is sound (or valid). So in the following case (A):

All birds are animals
Parrots are birds
Therefore parrots are animals

We can see that both premises are true and the reasoning is sound. But what about this one (B)?:

All lizards are cold blooded
Snails are cold blooded
Therefore snails are lizards

We can see that both premises are true but the conclusion doesn't follow logically from them, so the argument is invalid.

Now consider the follwing case (C):

All humans are greedy
Socrates is a human
Therefore Socrates is greedy

While realistically we might disagree with the first premise, if we *accept* it the conclusion follows logically out of the two premises so that technically the argument is valid.

Note: I am using the word 'valid' in the more specialised way it is used in philosophy, i.e. denoting a sound chain of reasoning. Valid is also used in a more general and looser way to mean reasonable, true or something I agree with, as in, 'I think you've made a valid point.'

The structure of syllogisms can be made clearer by representing them visually using patterns of circles. In all three examples in Figure 4.1 the largest circles represent the main or greatest categories or 'sets of things'. In example A, Birds is a subset of Animals and Parrots is a subset of Birds. In example B, we see at once that Lizards and Snails are subsets of Cold blooded things, but those subsets do not overlap. In example C, the patterns of circles is the same as in example A and logically the argument is valid if we accept that the subset of Humans exists within the greater category of Greedy things.

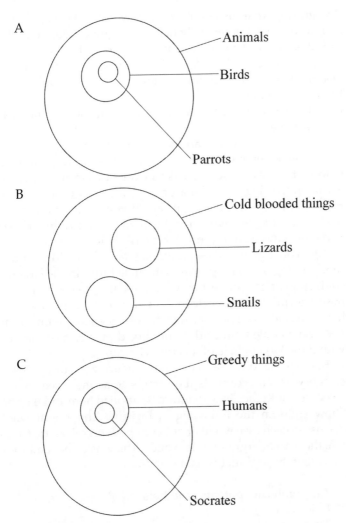

Figure 4.1 Syllogisms

Looking at syllogisms (and at deductive reasoning more generally) can become very complicated very quickly. The scope of this section means that we can only touch on a few main ideas (see the Bibliography for further pointers). However, even a 'first glance' benefits children's thinking skills in various ways:

- Recognising that using 'reasoning words' like so, thus and therefore doesn't necessarily make an argument sound (valid).
- Introducing or developing the notion of categories/sets and subsets. The use of circles bridges over into studying Venn Diagrams and offers children another kind of visual organiser for their thinking.
- Encouraging caution when confronted with terms such as all, always, never.
- Teaching that sentences are not necessarily reversible, i.e. that sometimes reversing a sentence preserves its truth and sometimes it doesn't. For example, 'All oaks are trees that grow from acorns' is true. Reversing it to, 'All acorns grow into oaks' maintains its truth. However, while we can say, 'If you have a cold then you have a runny nose' reversing it to, 'If you have a runny nose then you must have a cold' is not necessarily true.

    Tip: You can use these examples to help children practise representing logical arguments in circle form. In the case of the cold/runny nose connection we can see that 'people with runny noses' forms a larger category than 'people with colds' since having a cold is but one of a number of causes for getting a runny nose. So 'people with colds' would be drawn as a smaller circle within the larger circle of 'people with runny noses'.

    But what about the acorn/oak connection? In a sense the category of 'all acorns' is the same size as the category of 'all oaks', so could the circle diagram be applied here and if so how?
- Show children the following syllogisms. You might want to discuss in each case whether either or both premises are true and whether each argument is valid. Then ask the children to represent the arguments using circles.

    All women are potential mothers
    Julie is a woman
    Therefore Julie is a potential mother

    Ice cream is made out of cardboard
    All things made out of cardboard are good to eat
    Therefore ice cream is good to eat

Since sparrows have two legs
And since all birds have two legs
It follows that sparrows are birds

All red things are blue
All pink things are red
Therefore all pink things are blue

Tip: You might want to go for a little lie down after this!

BIG IDEAS

Traditionally philosophy deals with big ideas such as love, justice, identity, life and death, God and so on. But the point of teaching P4C is so that children can develop a robust and practical way of thinking about themselves, their relationships with others and how they might deal with the various issues and problems that crop up in their lives. In that sense philosophy is a very down-to-earth and pragmatic process for helping us all to become more rounded and mature individuals and happier, more useful members of society.

P4C within education follows the assertion of Socrates that philosophical thinking should be 'by the people, for the people'; that while it is indeed pursued to high levels of academic abstraction by professional philosophers, essentially it is a process that should be engaged in by ordinary people to deal with real world problems and difficulties.

Try these activities as a way of building the basic skills that will prepare children to take part in philosophical enquiries:

- Give a scrap of paper to every child in the class and ask them to write down the name of an object. Put the scraps in an envelope and draw out two at random – say, tomato and pen – now ask how many links the children can make between those two things. Repeat the activity a few more times. The linking game can be used as a 'mind warm-up' at the start of any lesson.

- *Same and Different.* This game also uses pairs of objects but the emphasis is slightly different. In this version, deliberately pick two objects that allow children to list both similarities and differences. So, for instance, 'crown' and 'treasure'. Both are made of precious metals and stones, but while the treasure signifies wealth in a general way, the crown specifically denotes the power of royalty.

- *Would You Rather…* For this activity, choose a theme and out of that generate three or four examples. So using the theme of 'ownership' you could ask the children to discuss whether they would rather own a big house, a small wood with a cabin, a kitten or a new smartphone. Under the theme of 'finding' ask whether the children would rather find ten thousand pounds, a living dinosaur, a jar of sweets that never empties or a doorway into tomorrow.

- *Linking game with concepts.* Show the children a picture like the one in Figure 4.2 that combines objects with concepts. The task is to pick two objects and one concept word and to link all three in a sentence or two. So, 'I pick the car and the jewels because they will give me greater freedom.'

Figure 4.2 Linking game with concepts

- *Scenarios.* Ask children to discuss scenarios like these:

  Would you give up half of what you own for a guaranteed extra five years of life?

  If you could become either much more intelligent or much better looking, which would you choose?

  You discover that your best friend has been cheating in a test. What would you do?

  Would you choose to become much better off in life if you knew that a stranger in another country would become that much worse off as a result?

  Tip: The Kids' Book of Questions by Gregory Stock (2004) contains many more examples.

CRAFTING QUESTIONS

We've already looked at different categories of questions, which we can take a step further in moving towards a full-blown philosophical enquiry. In the context of P4C the following guidelines are useful:

- Different types of questions produce different types of responses. (This seems obvious but has subtle implications.)
- Questions are useful even if there seems to be no absolute right answer. (In fact an interesting philosophical discussion could explore what the idea of a 'right answer' means!)
- Opinions sometimes count as perfectly acceptable answers (ideally, backed up with reasons).
- Questions can be framed precisely or more vaguely and both can be useful techniques for further understanding.

Traditionally in P4C the teacher is a 'facilitator', smoothing the way for the children to engage in a discussion. It is important that over time, having explicitly taught different skills and having guided the children through the process of enquiry, the teacher 'steps back', either becoming simply another member of the circle (usually in a P4C enquiry chairs are arranged in a circle. I explain to children that this is for the same reason that King Arthur chose a round table – everyone sitting there was equally valued) or sitting in the background just observing.

In your role as facilitator you can 'model the behaviour' by asking different kinds of questions that support the children's thinking and move an enquiry forward. For example:

- *Questions that seek more clarification.* Can you explain that more/ in a different way? What do you mean by that? Can you give me an example of that idea? Does anyone have a question about that idea?
- *Questions that explicitly ask for reasons and evidence.* How do we know that? Why do you think so? What is the evidence for saying that? Can you give your reasons for that opinion?
- *Questions that explore other viewpoints.* How else could we look at that? What would you say if someone suggested…? What do you think someone who disagreed with you might say? What is the difference between your view and the one that (Tony) just mentioned?
- *Questions that focus on implications and consequences.* What can we conclude/decide/say based on what you've just said? (How) does that view fit with what we said earlier? What would follow on from that? Is there a general rule or principle to support that idea? How could we test that idea to see if it worked/was true?
- *Questions about other questions and about the enquiry itself.* What kind of question do you think that is? How does that help us with the theme of our discussion? Where have we got to in our discussion so far? Are we closer to answering the question we started with? What other (kinds of) questions could we ask to keep exploring the issue?

During an enquiry all questions are asked in a spirit of mutual respect and a genuine wish to find an answer. There should be no element of personal criticism involved. The principle for children to bear in mind here is, 'Be merciless in searching for the truth but be merciful when it comes to other people.'

THE ENQUIRY PROCESS

While a philosophical enquiry is free flowing in itself (though keeping to the point of the initial question as far as possible), there is a step-by-step process that leads up to it. This is necessary so that the children's discussions are rich in ideas and incisive in their exploration of the chosen themes, as opposed to a simple exchange of views.

In preparing for an enquiry:

- *Offer a stimulus.* This can be a picture, a story, a video clip etc. The most useful and powerful stimulus will in some way highlight a 'big idea' like love, life and death, good and evil, identity etc. It might also incorporate 'tension' insofar as it could be controversial or at least support different viewpoints. A good stimulus will also be interesting in its own right so that it prompts children to think, talk and question.
- *Encourage first thoughts.* Allow children thinking time to reflect individually on their initial response to the stimulus. You can prompt them by asking them to consider what they felt about the stimulus, what they found interesting, puzzling, amusing or shocking about it. The philosopher/P4C teacher Jason Buckley suggests asking each child to write five words, phrases, opinions or ideas on separate scraps of paper. All the scraps are then placed within the enquiry circle as a 'concept pool' for the children to think about further.
- *Craft the searching questions.* Ideally it should be the children (usually working in groups) who create a menu of questions from which they can choose one for discussion. These questions should be 'juicy', ripe with potential for exploration. The writer and philosopher Stephen Law in his excellent *The Philosophy Files* (2000, 2003) bases his discussions on questions such as: What's real? Where do right and wrong come from? Does God exist? Could a machine think? Questions like these immediately

prompt a reaction and 'open the door' to further reflection. Notice that they are likely to evoke different opinions, prompt a search for clearer meanings and definitions, and lead to responses that can be justified by reasons. Questions whose answers can simply be looked up or ones that are purely speculative, such as 'Do ghosts exist?' (however, if the question was 'Are ghosts real?' that would open the door to an enquiry about what 'real' means), will not make for meaty philosophical enquiries.

- *Air the questions.* Ask the children to examine the questions to see if they will actually lead to a philosophical enquiry. It is helpful if the group that created the questions talks about them briefly, explaining why their question is interesting. Encourage children to come up with questions *about* the question they are looking at; this is a good test of whether or not that question is juicy enough.

- *Vote on the questions.* Ask children to choose the question they would like to discuss. This might be a straight show of hands, or children can be asked to go and stand beside the question they like. My preference is for a 'blind vote' where children close their eyes then put up their hands, as this stops children just going along with what their friends want.

- *First exchange of views.* Good questions for enquiry will provoke a strong opinion that children will be eager to talk about. Let the children get into pairs and simply tell one another briefly how they feel about the issue. They are more likely to listen patiently when the enquiry proper is going on if they have had this first chance to air their views.

- *Launch the enquiry.* The discussion now opens up to the whole group. The enquiry can be launched in various ways:
  - Find out which pupils have a very strong opinion ('six' on a 1–6 scale). Pick one to kick off the enquiry, then follow with someone who has an equally strong though opposite viewpoint.
  - Ask the group whose question was chosen to explain their view.
  - If the question can (initially) be answered yes or no, get pupils to stand either side of a yes-no line, though they can only take up their position if they have at least one reason to back up their opinion.

- *Develop the enquiry.* This is the heart of the session, where questions are asked, reasons given, examples and counter-examples offered etc. It is especially important here that you consider yourself as just one of the community of enquirers (rather than the adult in the room leading the discussion). Having said that, you can gently guide the enquiry by:
  - letting each speaker choose the next as far as possible
  - encouraging priority for those who have spoken less (but want to contribute now)
  - suggesting to those children who tend to ramble to make their point as briefly as possible
  - encouraging the children to look at each other as they speak rather than at you.

  Tip: Instead of getting children who want to speak to put up their hand (which can be tiring after a while), you can suggest that they place a hand palm upwards on the thigh.

  Sometimes discussion will stall. There are various ways of dealing with this.
  - Get the children back into groups for a quick brainstorming of further questions or an exchange of views.
  - Ask a dumb question or express a controversial view yourself to prompt further reaction.
  - Ask for someone to agree or disagree with the last speaker backed by a reason. Repeat the process until the enquiry builds up momentum again.
- *Make time for last thoughts.* Pace the enquiry so that children have some opportunity to decide where they stand on the issue now. Ask them to indicate whether they have changed their minds, whether they have kept the same view but feel more strongly about it now, whether they have had a useful insight or whether they are more confused now (implying that the issue is more complex than they first thought and requires further consideration).
- *Do a review.* Ask the children to reflect on the session itself; on what went well and not so well. It is important here to bear in mind that pointing out what didn't go well does not imply any criticism or negative judgement of any of the community. This is also an ideal time for children to look at their skills ticklist (see p. 84) and ask the kinds of questions mentioned in 'How did it

go?' on page **45**. Explicitly ask the children how this enquiry was different from/better than the last one. What 'moves' were made (see 'The Right Moves' below) that helped the discussion? Ask children to sum up for themselves (perhaps in a thinking journal) what they think they have learned from the enquiry.

• *Anticipate the next enquiry.* Sometimes during a discussion a really juicy 'side issue' crops up which could form the theme of the next enquiry. Or you might ask children to look for what they think will be a useful stimulus.

What is important is that P4C enquiries should not just be 'fitted in' ad hoc to the timetable or take place once in a blue moon. The thinking and communicating skills that children will develop during their discussions bring positive benefits right across the curriculum. As such, enquiries should happen regularly and lie at the heart of the children's learning experience.

THE RIGHT MOVES

'Moves' – the tactics of enquiry – often take the form of questions. They are the tools and techniques we use to think with and reflect the core skills we want children to develop in P4C. As the facilitator of an enquiry you can demonstrate these moves yourself by joining in with the discussion, asking children to use particular moves and pointing out to a child when she has used a move (another version of 'making the thinking explicit').

Commonly used moves are:

• *Clarifying.* So can you tell me more about what you mean? What exactly do you mean by that? How would you define that word?
• *Making connections.* So how does that link to the other point(s) we made?
• *Highlighting consequences.* So what follows from that? What could happen then?
• *Contradicting.* We've got two opposite viewpoints here. Can you tell me why you think you are right? Can anyone say more about

how they can't both be right? Could both viewpoints be right and if so how?

- *Defining.* Will you explain that more clearly? What do you mean by that word/idea?
- *Exploring distinctions.* So how are those examples/ideas different?
- *Finding evidence.* How could you back up your view? What supports your idea? What reasons will make that opinion stronger?
- *Finding exceptions.*
- *Giving examples and counterexamples.*
- *Generalising.* Is that always the case/always true?
- *Highlighting implications.* So does that also mean… What might follow from what you've just said?
- *Particularising.* How might that apply to you/us/this school/ where we live etc.?
- *Restating.* How else could we say/explain that?
- *Seeing the overview or general principles.* What's the big idea behind what we've said?
- *Probing uncertainty.* How is it that we can't be sure about that?

MORAL DILEMMAS

An important element of philosophy is the notion of morality – our sense of right and wrong and how we as a species possess it. Any exploration of the topic must involve a consideration of values and beliefs. Here are some scenarios to stimulate discussion. They can also be used as starting points for following the step-by-step process of launching philosophical enquiries with your class.

Tip: There are some excellent YouTube clips of P4C in action. If you are especially interested in doing philosophy with young children, search for the sessions with the philosophy teacher Sara Stanley.

1 You see your friend cheating in a written test. You know that if anyone is caught cheating the whole class will be punished and shamed. But you also know that your friend is likely to fail the test if he or she doesn't cheat.

Would you tell on your friend?

What would you do if, knowing you were likely to fail the test too, your friend offered to share answers?

What if your friend's Mum was very ill in hospital and quite likely to die?

2   You are involved in an accident aboard a ship. The ship quickly sinks but you escape with eleven other people in a life raft. The raft is now fully laden. As you discuss what to do, a thirteenth person swims towards you crying out for help. That person grabs hold of the raft, but it begins to tilt dangerously, risking you all.

Now what would you do?

Would your feelings or decision be different if the person was a young girl?

Would your feelings or decision be different if the person was elderly?

3   It is the future. The human population of Earth has increased so much that we are in danger of extinction due to huge wars over water and food. The World Government suggests that if everyone over thirty agreed to be killed painlessly, the human race would survive and life would quickly become better for everyone.

Do you agree with the World Government's plan in principle?

Would you agree with it if the age limit were different?

Whatever the age limit, would you make any exceptions to the rule? Why?

CHAPTER 5

Jumpstart thinking and problem solving in emotional resourcefulness

CORE SKILLS FOR EMOTIONAL RESOURCEFULNESS

Because the mind and the body are inextricably connected, what and how we think has a profound effect on what we feel and how we manage our emotions. A further benefit of developing thinking skills in children is that they learn to have greater control over their own feelings and therefore how they regard themselves and how they relate to other people. Another aspect of the notion of 'resourcefulness' in this context is that we can think of our feelings as *resources* in the same way that we can call memory and imagination resources – sources of power and potential that we can return to again and again.

Throughout this book we've emphasised the core skills of noticing and questioning. These dispositions are just as important in learning to deal more effectively with feelings, which from the outset require an awareness of self and an awareness of others. Here are some ideas for helping children to recognise and begin to work more purposefully with their emotions:

- Look at the origins for the names of some common feelings. Are the same roots used in other words? What connections can you make? For instance 'happy' comes through Middle English from *hap*, which also crops up in 'happen' (event, chance, fortune), 'hapless' (unlucky) and 'haphazard' (chance, accident). 'Anger' comes from Old Norse *angr* (grief, trouble), akin to the Old English *enge* (narrow) from the Latin *angere* (to strangle – linked here to angina, which shares the same root).

- Make a longer list of feelings. Separate them out into those which are pleasant and those which are not. Draw a line on the board, mark one end positive and the other negative, and ask the children to discuss where along the line the feelings should be placed (with more powerful emotions towards the ends and milder emotions towards the middle).

  Extend the activity by using the Emotion Matrix (Figure 5.1), introducing the idea of how commonly we experience different emotions as well as thinking about their strength or degree.

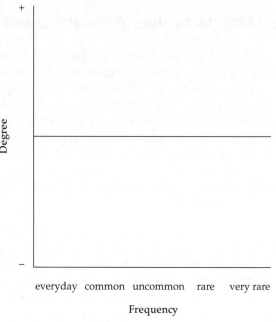

everyday common uncommon rare very rare

Frequency

Figure 5.1 Emotion matrix

- *Name that feeling.* Split the class into pairs. Ask one child in each pair to think of a feeling and mime it as best he can, including body posture and facial expression. The other child in the pair must try to guess the feeling. Then the roles reverse.
- *Mirrors.* As above, but this time as one child mimes an emotion, the other has to copy him.

- *Voice tones.* Use a sentence like, 'I'd like a packet of crisps please.' Write the names of some feelings on scraps of paper and put these in an envelope. One child draws out a scrap (without showing anyone else) and has to say the sentence in the tone of voice that matches the chosen emotion. Extend the activity by asking children to notice the different tonal qualities of the various emotions – pitch, volume, timbre, speed etc.
- *'Happiness is…'* Choose a positive emotion such as happiness to begin with. Ask the children, perhaps working in small groups, to come up with examples that complete the sentence 'Happiness is a trip to the funfair/unexpectedly finding a sweet in your pocket/a sunny weekend at the seaside', etc.
- *Positive memories.* Simply ask the children to sit quietly. Tell them to relax and breathe calmly, then to deliberately bring a pleasant memory to mind and, as they do so, notice that associated feelings also rise. This highlights the fact that thoughts and feelings are linked.
- *Note:* Sometimes a child, for whatever reason, will have an unhappy/unpleasant memory. Make it clear to the class at the outset that any child can opt out of any activity if he is not comfortable.

'AS I THINK, SO I AM' – NOTICING METAPHORS

Metaphors (and other figurative comparisons) powerfully shape the way we regard ourselves, each other and the world. Even though metaphors wield such influence they often go unnoticed in the language, which is crammed, riddled, laden and packed full-to-bursting with them. Because thoughts are linked to feelings, the metaphors we apply to ourselves largely determine how we feel.

I was running a creative writing workshop at a school once, when a boy came up to me and said that he couldn't do the work. When I asked him why he said, 'Because I'm thick.' I replied, 'Well pretend you're thin for a while and come and tell me when you've finished the story.' He laughed, went off and wrote the story. I admit to being surprised at the effect my off-the-cuff comment had on him, but on reflection realised that it had influenced that pupil positively because:

- it showed him another way of looking at the word 'thick'
- it amused him
- it used 'when' as a presupposition of success, so that subconsciously he registered my expectation that he would inevitably succeed in the task.

Talking of expectations, the deputy head who sat in on the workshop told me afterwards that years before, as a pupil, he had been going through a bad patch. His English teacher, who was about to retire, said to him, 'I'll be keeping in touch with news at the school. I expect great things from you.' The deputy head said that those few simple words had changed his life and set him on a career in education.

Here are some ways to help children to recognise the metaphors embedded in their language:

- As soon as you or they spot one, flip it round to make a positive opposite:
  - thick/thin
  - I've let myself down/I'll lift myself up
  - I've hit a brick wall/I've sailed over the wall
  - it's like I'm battling with myself/I've made friends with myself
  - it's an uphill struggle/it's a downhill ride
  - up the river without a paddle/up the river with a powerboat.
  It is important to realise that children are not required to *try and believe* these modified comparisons. The point of the task is to notice them and to change them consciously and deliberately.

Be aware too of the metaphors that help to form the 'lexicon of schooling' where children are streamed, set, graded, tasked, pushed and stretched; where there are levels, league tables and targets; where youngsters must not slip back, fall by the wayside or get left behind; and where we are all urged 'to fight and run in the global race'.

- Proverbs are a rich source of figurative statements about people and their view of the world. Make a selection and ask the children to discuss what they mean and if/to what degree they are true. For example:

> It never rains but it pours.
> No gain without pain.
> The proof of the pudding is in the eating.
> Time is money.
> What's done can't be undone.
> When you're going down the hill everyone will give you a push.
> Who knows most says least.
> You can't get blood out of a stone.
> You can't teach an old dog new tricks.
> And my very favourite, 'As you butter your bread, so must you lie on it.'

- *The animal connection.* Many metaphors that we apply to ourselves come from the animal kingdom. Ask the children to pick a selection of animals and list some of their attributes. Looking at common similes makes a good start, for example: as brave as a lion, as wise as an owl etc. Each child then selects positive characteristics from several creatures to apply to himself; children can even invent and draw new animals to depict their ideas.

IT NEVER RAINS BUT IT POURS

There are many ways in which our imaginations can 'run away with us'. When it comes to dealing with feelings (or not) these unhelpful ways of thinking are known as cognitive distortions. They include:

- *All-or-nothing thinking.* This is where we look at the world in black and white. If something isn't just right then it's totally ruined.
- *Emotionally weighted thinking.* This is where negative emotions colour our whole view of the world. Such thinking is reinforced if we label ourselves – 'I'm thick', 'I'm a loser', 'I'll never be good enough' etc.

- *Filtering.* This is where we pick out from our whole range of experiences those which support negative, self-limiting beliefs.
- *Generalising.* This is where we take a general view based on one or two experiences (which might themselves be false assumptions or misinterpretations, for example, 'I've noticed two people today laughing while they look at me. Why does everyone laugh at me? What's wrong with me?').
- *Mind reading.* This is where we think we know what other people are thinking about us and use these suspicious to jump to negative conclusions.
- *Taking it personally.* This could be in terms of criticism, blame, someone else's anger etc., whether or not these are justified.
- *What-if worrying.* This is where we create negative future scenarios often without thinking that these haven't happened yet and maybe never will; nor do we usually plan strategically in case such events come to pass.
- *Wishful thinking.* This is where we yearn to be different or for things to change, yet wallow in these thoughts rather than take action on the matter.

Cognitive distortions can overlap like a Venn diagram and reinforce each other, so adding to the problem. The general – and often very effective – solution to such ways of thinking is firstly to *notice that they are going on*. Once we recognise these habits of thought we can consciously and deliberately do something about them. Ways of dealing with negative thoughts and feelings include:

- *Direct positive action.* If I'm not happy with the way things are, then what can I do to change them? (A wise old saying tells us that to solve a problem in life, change yourself and/or change your circumstances.)
- *Balancing things up.* 'One the one hand I didn't do that very well, but on the other hand I've done it successfully lots of times in the past.'
- *Speculation.* 'Maybe those people were laughing at me, but maybe they were just in a good mood. Or maybe someone just said something funny, or maybe…'
- *'How do I know?'* Thinking about where the evidence is to be found often reveals that it doesn't exist and also highlights the

false assumptions we've made and the shaky conclusions we've reached.
- *Take as you find.* Doing this, rather than pre-judging an issue or person, can powerfully limit the effect of negative thinking.

You can find more examples of cognitive distortions and how to deal with them in my book *Self-Intelligence* (1999). I would also highly recommend Dale Carnegie's *How to Stop Worrying and Start Living* (1972), a book which changed my outlook on life during my teenage years!

WHAT WE THINK WE KNOW

This is a quick and easy activity that helps children to recognise assumptions and how easy it is sometimes to make them.

Use a picture like the one in Figure 5.2 and ask the children to discuss in groups what they think is going on. What judgements do they make about the characters in the picture? What 'clues' did they notice that led them to those conclusions?

Figure 5.2 What's going on?

Once the groups have reported back their ideas, point out the following:

- Stereotyping (a kind of generalising) is an easy trap to fall into.
- 'Reasoning words' such as because, so and therefore do not in themselves indicate the strength of a reason or even necessarily support it. Maybe one of the groups said, 'The man sitting down is obviously showing off because of his posh clothes and his big cigar and just the way he's sitting…' Point out that he might in fact be poor, using the last of his money to hire a suit to visit his daughter, trying to persuade her to invest in a sure-fire business venture.
- Draw attention to rhetorical words such as obviously, surely, clearly etc. In this case it is not obvious that the man is showing off.
- Ask the children to come up with more possible explanations for the scenario.

    Tip: You don't need pictures for this activity; suitable text will do just as well, such as, '"I really want to feel that you're making an effort for me, Gillian," said Miss Nellis, turning to look briefly at the passenger sitting in the back seat.'

VALUES

Values form the emotional bedrock on which we stand, giving rise to our beliefs and influencing our judgements, decisions and actions. Helping children to become more aware of and reflective about what they hold to be valuable is a key aspect of developing their emotional resourcefulness.

In discussing values, point out to children that giving them some thought:

- helps us to cope when things become difficult. If I value a friendship then I will work to preserve it after a quarrel or disagreement. If I value determination then I can remind myself of that if a task seems arduous, boring or frustrating;

- makes us more aware of why we are happy (or not). Often enough unhappiness occurs when actions and values don't match. Once such a mismatch has been recognised, solutions usually become clearer;
- allows us to gain insights into why we are behaving the way we do. As a teacher, reflect on the way certain children behave for you and for others. What is it they value that might account for this? Reflect on your own behaviour in different situations and how this connects with what you value – doing this will help you to guide children's thinking as and when you ask them to do the same.

Respecting the values of others even if you disagree with them is in itself a value. Quite often when I visit schools to talk about my books I'm asked, 'Are you rich? Are you famous? Have you won any awards?' While wealth, fame and recognition might be pleasant, these things are not as important to me as the satisfaction of tackling and completing a writing project: I would write even if I knew my work would never be published or earn me a penny. In answering children therefore I like to say, 'I'm lucky. I just about make a living being a writer but more importantly I make a life from it.' And that's the key question: what's important to you? What do you want to make of your life? Here are some activities to tackle these questions:

- Ask the children to come up with a list of values. These needn't be ones that they themselves hold, although it is likely that in many cases they will. That being so, ask each child to pick the values that are important to her and link them to a decision she has made or an action that she has taken. In other words, making a direct link between value and behaviour.
- Discuss the 'noble qualities' embodied in the hero figure in films and books. What makes a hero? Do the same values exist in people who are heroic in real life? Can you be heroic in one kind of situation but not in another? Does that diminish you as a hero?
- Revisit examples of moral dilemmas. How are the children's opinions (and actions if they were actually in those situations) linked to their values?

POSITIVE PURPOSES

If you put your hand against a very hot radiator you soon know about it; the pain kicks in and you snatch your hand away. The pain itself is unpleasant but its purpose is a positive one, to make you react quickly and so minimise the damage to your hand.

The principle of positive purposes can be applied to feelings too. Some feelings are not pleasant but they are purposeful – there are reasons behind them, even if at the moment we might not know what they are or perhaps just have an inkling. Being willing to accept that apparently negative emotions have a positive underlying purpose is the first step towards being able to use such feelings as a resource.

Work with positive emotions first. Ask children to think of an incident that evoked a pleasant emotion, like laughing after someone told a joke or feeling a sense of excitement just before going on holiday. Encourage examples where the incident-emotion link is obvious.

Now work with hypothetical situations involving apparently negative emotions. Prepare a few examples beforehand to illustrate the point. So, for instance, Mrs Stephens might become angry at seeing one child bullying another. Point out that the anger doesn't 'feel nice' but that its positive purpose is to highlight the strength of Mrs Stephens' disapproval of bullying. (It might also be the case that she feels so strongly because she herself was bullied as a child. Sometimes we experience unpleasant emotions for no obvious consciously recognised reasons. Rather, the reasons are rooted in incidents that we have forgotten. When this happens 'trying hard' not to feel like that doesn't usually work, but there are other strategies that we can use to help resolve the matter, which we'll look at later.)

Extend this activity by listing more unpleasant emotions such as envy, regret, irritation, nervousness etc. Use a fictitious character such as Mrs Stephens. Ask the children to think of a situation where she felt one of those emotions and then to reflect on what 'positive message' the feeling could be conveying.

Tip: Notice that we are not asking children to think about unpleasant emotions or upsetting situations that they have experienced. The hope is that having understood the idea of positive purposes children will apply the principle to themselves.

SAFE HAVEN

This is an ancient technique that brings the following benefits:

- it develops the ability to feel calm and relaxed at will
- it increases concentration span
- it develops the ability to internalise the point of attention and to notice and modify thoughts (metacognition).

The idea is simply to imagine a pleasant place and to hold the image in mind for a period of time. Each child can choose his own pleasant place. It may be based on somewhere real, somewhere entirely made up or a mixture of both. In preparing children for the task:

- Ask them to sit comfortably. If they are sitting on chairs then they should sit straight but not stiffly and, as far as possible, without fidgeting. They can either close their eyes or look at a blank spot on the wall or floor.
- Do an 'all over relax'. Start at the head and move the attention slowly downwards. Notice any areas of tension – frowning, tense shoulders, taut stomach muscles etc. – and deliberately relax.
- Ask the children now to be aware of their breathing. If they are breathing quickly or shallowly, ask them to change that to slower, deeper breaths. Point out that as they relax and slow the breath they will feel calmer and more settled.
- Now get them to begin imagining their pleasant place (you might have asked them to give this some thought beforehand). Ask them to notice what's nearby, what's in the distance. Ask

them to notice colours, sounds, scents and even textures. Prompt them to notice how pleasant it feels just to be thinking of such a place.

Initially the visualisation need last only a minute or two. Some children will find it hard to concentrate even for that short time – you'll notice some looking around, fidgeting more etc. Don't try to force them into the task; as long as they're not distracting anyone else that's fine.

Like any thinking skill this one grows stronger with practice, so it is advisable to do the activity at least once a week. Gradually increase the 'quiet time' to around five minutes. Suggest to the children that they can add more details to their pleasant place each time they go there.

When children are more proficient at the task, ask them to imagine some small object that they find there. Encourage them to visualise this in as much detail as possible. After the quiet time, invite those who are willing to describe their object. Suggest to everyone that whenever they imagine that object, all the good feelings associated with being in their pleasant place will rise in them again.

Further suggest at some point that whenever a child feels angry or upset she can have some thinking time to go to her pleasant place, leaving all the bad feelings outside. After spending just a few minutes there, she can come back feeling calmer yet stronger and much more easily able to deal with the situation that caused the problem.

WHAT SHAPE IS THAT FEELING?

Here is an effective technique for modifying unpleasant/self limiting feelings. It is based on the two principles

- that thoughts, feelings and physical reactions are linked; and
- that what we consciously think about we subconsciously react to.

Imagine a child comes to you feeling upset. Of course you might want to investigate the cause of the problem, but work on the feeling directly first. Say to the child, 'If that feeling of upset had a shape, what would it be?'

If the child says she doesn't know reply by saying, 'Pretend you do and tell me when you know' or, 'Just make it up as you go along.'

Once the child has given you the shape ask about the size, colour, weight and texture of the feeling. Encourage the child to 'mould out' the feeling with her hands (although most children will use body language spontaneously anyway). Continue by saying, 'Squeeze that feeling. What happens? Pretend you can scratch it – what's beneath the surface? Does it have a smell? Tell me about that…'

Finally ask where inside the body the feeling is located.

The child has now created a concrete metaphor of the feeling causing the problem. Tell her that now she is going to change everything about it, following your cues. Move through this at a brisk pace and ask the child to tell you about each change she makes – shape, size, colour, weight, texture and scent. Then get her to locate the feeling somewhere else – a little humour works well so on the tip of the nose, on a kneecap, on the end of the big toe.

Now say, 'OK, swish it away and it's gone.' Then ask the child to look at something colourful in the room. This tactic is called a 'break state': you have broken her state of concentration once you have taken her through the process of modifying a negative feeling. That acts like a mental full stop, in effect letting the child know that she can do the same thing for herself whenever she wishes.

On one occasion a teacher rather cynically said that this technique was make-believe. Quite so – we were making the belief that the child could have greater control over her emotions.

THE WORLD INSIDE

This extends the idea of working metaphorically with feelings. Mark out a large circle on a tabletop and tell the class that it represents the mind of a person (yet to be chosen). Anything that is put inside the circle tells us something about the thoughts and feelings going on inside that person.

Give some examples. A camera might go in the circle because the person actually wants a camera for his birthday, or it could represent his desire to travel and create a photographic record of his adventures. A brass weight could mean he feels depressed at the moment or has a lot on his mind. Abstract shapes like those we looked at on pages **9** and **32** are also useful inclusions – what could it be, what does it remind you of?

The person in question could be made up from scratch, in which case invent a name, a physical description and a timeline, or you could take a character from literature or film to work on.

You can combine this activity with the circle game (p. **42**). Large objects are things that are foremost in our character's mind; objects placed close together are closely connected as far as our character is concerned etc.

Initially children might give you very literal interpretations about objects chosen to go in the circle. Tim might choose an orange because the character likes oranges! In time, though, children will understand the power of metaphor – the orange might come to represent the character's desire to live healthily or visit an exotic land.

In terms of literacy this technique helps children to create characters for their stories that have depth. The game can also be used analytically – having read a story, what would you put inside the circle-mind of the hero, the villain...? And what are the reasons behind your choices?

When children become more familiar with the technique they can apply it to themselves. At this stage point out that *choosing* which items go into the circle and how they are positioned is very important. Also suggest that things can change. Ask children to create a circle-mind for themselves as they will be at some time in the future, when a problem has been solved, a project successfully completed etc.

ANCHORS AWAY!

This is an elegant and powerful technique found in NLP (Neuro Linguistic Programming. This explores and exploits the connections between our neurology, the language we use and our patterns of behaviour. As an approach to personal development it has its critics, but I have found some of its ideas and techniques to be effective. You must of course judge for yourself). An 'anchor' is a link that is made between a desired behaviour and something that is under your conscious control.

Here is an example of an anchor: when the school bell rings at the end of break time children (ideally) line up ready to come indoors. There is a link between the bell and the behaviour of the children. We can say that this is a positive auditory anchor. Similarly, a story corner is a positive spatial anchor – children come to associate that space (and maybe that particular time of day) with the enjoyment of listening to a story.

A variation of the spatial anchor idea is for you to designate certain spots in the room where you stand when you want the children to behave in a certain way. So you might have a spot where you stand each time you introduce a new topic and you want the children to pay attention, be receptive to new ideas, ask searching questions etc. You can have another spot where you stand when you want children to get into the 'creative flow' and come up with fresh thoughts, insights and suggestions. Also try a 'discipline spot', a place where you stand when the class becomes too noisy and/or you need to give the children a pep talk.

Don't tell the children about your anchor points, as they operate subliminally. That is, the link between you standing *there* and them behaving in a certain way is made at a subconscious level.

However, some anchors can be consciously triggered. If a child is right-handed, ask him to rub his thumb and little finger together on his left hand (and vice versa for left-handed children). This is something he must decide to do (rather than doing it inadvertently). Now suggest that each time he feels pleased with something he's accomplished or even if he's just in a good mood, he can run thumb and finger together to establish the movement as a positive tactile anchor. In effect he is reminding himself that those good feelings are there and can be enjoyed. Also the activity is cumulative; the positive feelings will become stronger over time when the anchor is triggered.

As a further benefit, if, for whatever reason, the child experiences unpleasant feelings he can trigger the anchor to access positive emotions to help modify, balance out or eliminate the negative ones.

CONTROL ROOM

The control room technique is a further visualisation to help children 'turn down' unpleasant feelings and increase the effects of positive ones. The activity can either be done entirely in the imagination or children can be invited to draw their impressions.

Ask them to imagine a control room inside their minds. This is where all the things that go on inside them are monitored and controlled, including feelings and thoughts that they don't know they're thinking (subconscious thoughts). However they imagine this room, it will be a very busy place with lots of measuring instruments, computer interfaces, hard disc drives for storage and so on. Also suggest that they can notice a number of very efficient, friendly looking technicians and assistants who are making sure that everything runs smoothly. These assistants are there to help whenever needed.

Now ask each child to decide on a reason for visiting the control room. It might be to make a good feeling last longer or grow stronger, or to get rid of a bad feeling.

Inside the room there is a machine that is in charge of the thoughts and feelings the child wants to work with. The child now imagines going to that machine and noticing all of its dials, switches, buttons, levers and monitor screens. Ask the child to pay attention to the way the controls are set and any 'readings' from the screens and dials.

Explain that it is likely the child will 'just know what to do' to reset the controls on that machine, but if not one of those helpful assistants will be nearby to advise.

While this visualisation is going on, try to ensure that the children are not distracted. Ideally they need to concentrate on the task without interruption. Having said that, the visualisation only lasts for two or three minutes.

Suggest that having reset the machine, the child mentally thanks the assistants and technicians for doing such a good job.

If children want to draw their machines then they should do 'before' and 'after' versions.

Tip: This activity works well with 'The World Inside' (p. 114), where children can rearrange the items in their mind-circle, take something out, put in something new etc.

CHANGE THE MEMORY

The mind is not like a camera that captures what is 'really out there' in terms of recording objectively. Our subconscious 'map' of memories – that incredible network of understandings and meanings in our heads – is based upon our interpretations of events, and not in isolation but in association with many other experiences we've had. We 'make sense' of the world in a unique and subjective way.

That said, when memories become conscious we tend to remember these incidents in the same way each time. If, for example, I keep recalling an argument I had with someone then I will always be looking at that person through my own eyes, seeing the incident in colour, hearing the person's voice sound the same and so on. And of course the same feelings rise inside me because of this. (That's how *my* mind works. Other people may recall images in black and white, sounds may be much more clearly remembered, or the whole incident might be witnessed from a third-person perspective. However an event is recalled, the technique of changing the memory is often very effective).

The technique can work on a one-to-one basis or with a whole class. Here are some ideas for using it with children:

- Ask the children to remember a pleasant experience and to notice *how* the recollection is structured – colour/black and white, sounds clear/fuzzy, first-person/third-person perspective. Because it is an enjoyable memory, once the children have noticed how they're remembering get them to enhance those aspects. If a child remembers in colour, can those colours become a little more vivid now? Can the child hear words that were spoken more clearly? As a result of all this, will the pleasant feelings become even stronger now?
- A way to work with less pleasant experiences is to ask the children to choose a memory that they didn't like, to notice one aspect of it – and then change it. (If you like, you can use the 'What Shape is That Feeling' technique (p. **112**) to diminish negative emotions prior to revisiting the memory itself.) If the child is remembering from a first-person perspective (through his own eyes), get him to imagine floating out of himself so that he can *look at himself* in the experience he is remembering. Work through several aspects of the memory in this way.
- Now have some fun. If there's another person in the memory that made the experience unpleasant, create an amusing change. Make that person turn green/pink/bright yellow; shrink the person to the size of a Chihuahua; change the person's voice to sound like Donald Duck; make that person deflate like a balloon with a little wheezy whistling sound. In other words, use your imagination.

- Follow up this work by having the children deliberately recall the experience in the modified way. Eventually the changes will become embedded and a child might discover he needs to make an effort to remember the unpleasant incident in its original form.

Note of caution: It is not advisable to deal with serious or traumatic memories in this way, nor should children be told to 'try not to remember' unpleasant events; that can simply lead to the suppression of issues that need to be addressed and resolved. If in any doubt professional help and advice should be sought.

TIME TRAVELLER

The power of the imagination can also be used to clarify intentions, charge up aspirations with positive emotional energy and utilise the resource of memory more effectively:

Ask the children to think of something they would realistically like to achieve in the future.

Having done that, get them to think about what positive personal qualities they think they'd need to make their plan succeed.

Then give some thought to the steps they think they'd need to take to increase the likelihood of success.

Now ask the children to imagine themselves either carrying out their plan and/or having reached that point in their lives when they've succeeded. Say to them, 'Think about how you'll look and act and think and feel when you've achieved what you set out to do.' Encourage them to make that mental impression as vivid as possible and to experience and enjoy 'all of the good feelings that go with it.'

Tip: If you've shown the children how to create a positive personal anchor (p. **115**) this would be the time for them to use it.

An extension of this technique is to get the children to imagine their successful future selves giving their 'now selves' encouragement and words of advice. This is based on the principle that *we know more than we think we know*: that our subconscious resource of memory contains useful information and creative power that enhances our conscious ability to form intentions, consider options, reach conclusions and make decisions. Such 'whole mind thinking' can be enormously effective.

WHERE DO YOU STAND?

One of the key elements of a successful philosophical enquiry is to respect the views of others even if you strongly disagree with them. The important word here is 'respect' which is 'the act of looking back' or looking again. The same idea surfaces in the field of emotional resourcefulness where we pay respect to what other people think (in terms of listening carefully to and considering what they say), but also looking again at our own opinions and why we come to hold them.

Help children to evaluate where they stand on various issues in the following ways:

- Pick a topic that most if not all children are likely to have an opinion about, for example, 'The more homework you get the more successful you will be in life.'
- Ask the children to jot down their immediate response to that assertion, including how they *feel* about it. Then have them reflect on whether the feeling is supported by any reasons that they thought about before they wrote. If any child did this, invite them to air those reasons now.
- Encourage the children to question the statement. Developing this habit again dampens the tendency to make a knee jerk reflex and/or overreact and helps to match strength of feeling with strength of reasoning. Questions could include:
  - How far does 'more' go? If I was made to do six hours of homework a night would that lead to the benefits suggested by the statement?

- Do you mean homework from many different subjects?
- What if the amount of homework I got meant that I couldn't study other things that I want to pursue as a career, such as sport or playing a musical instrument?
- What exactly do you mean by 'successful'?
- What do you mean by 'in life'? Are you suggesting that more homework is linked with being more successful in relationships, for example?

• Show children examples of questionnaires, many of which employ a scale ranging from 'I strongly agree' to 'I strongly disagree'. Either use the same statement as before or choose another, such as, 'All work and no play makes Jack a dull boy.'

Make sure the children understand what this means then ask them to decide where on the scale they would position themselves: I strongly disagree/I disagree/I have no opinion/I agree/I strongly agree.

Again ask them to consider reasons and frame any questions they would use to analyse the statement – for example whether a hobby that one loves and puts a lot of time and effort into would count as work.

In the case of the examples above, how can we reconcile the idea that homework equals success with the idea that too much work makes you 'dull'? Ask children to consider whether their response to the first statement matches or is congruent with their response to the second.

• Extend the work you've done so far by showing children how *mediation* works. Mark out a line about twelve feet long on the floor and pick a situation that can be hypothetical for the purposes of showing the technique but which could happen.

Invent two characters, say Tony and Tanzie, and a situation that's causing conflict, such as: Tony and Tanzie sit at the same table in class. When Tony is trying to think something through he mutters to himself and this is constantly distracting for Tanzie, who finds it impossible to get on with her work.

Ask two children to role play these characters and then get them to stand at each end of the line. The aim of the technique is for Tony and Tanzie to reach a compromise by making concessions to the other person. So Tony might suggest trying to mutter more quietly. If Tanzie thinks this is a generous or helpful concession then she invites Tony to take a big step towards her along the line. If she thinks it's not a very useful suggestion but still acceptable she invites Tony to take a little step forward. If she won't accept the suggestion then Tony has to stay where he is.

But whatever the outcome, now Tanzie has to make a suggestion. She might say, 'Well if I'm really trying to concentrate I'll sit away from you. But if your muttering isn't distracting me much I'll remain at the table with our friends.' Depending on how Tony feels about that he will either invite Tanzie to step forward a lot, a little or not at all.

Emphasise that the children's suggestions and concessions have to be reasonable and offered in a way that is respectful of the other person's feelings. For Tony to say, 'Oh just get over it!' would be completely unacceptable.

While Tony and Tanzie are negotiating, other children can offer suggestions for them to consider. The activity ends when Tony and Tanzie are close enough on the line to shake hands.

- A variation of the mediation game is 'Give and Take'. This can involve more than two children. Pick a topic such as increased building of houses on green belt sites. Ask each child in the group to role play a different faction or view involved in this issue – a property developer, a member of the Campaign to Protect Rural England, someone struggling to get on the property ladder, a local resident etc.

As appropriate, discuss the topic with the whole class first before splitting the children into groups. Ask the children in each group to position themselves around the table in a way that reflects their viewpoint. The developer might choose to sit opposite the member of the CPRE for instance.

Each child has a number of scraps of paper. Pick one child (faction) to begin by offering a concession. The developer might say, 'OK I'll make one in four of the houses I build affordable homes.' He then writes that on a scrap of paper and puts it in the middle of the table. Whoever accepts that concession writes it out on a scrap of paper for themselves. So the first-time buyer might accept the offer but maybe the CPRE representative won't.

Now another faction has to offer a concession. The CPRE rep might say, 'I won't object if you halve the size of your development and build a local school.' Again the first-time buyer might take that concession but maybe the developer won't.

As far as possible, every faction (player) in the game must offer concessions. This might mean modifying previously offered/accepted concessions. The activity concludes when enough give-and-take has gone on for a generally accepted compromise to be reached.

DEAR DIARY

Keeping a diary brings many benefits and the idea itself can be used flexibly:

- Write down a short description of one thing you've seen today or this week that you would like to remember in ten years' time.
- Write down the most important question you've asked recently, or heard someone else ask. Why did you pick that particular question?
- Keep a diary based on a character you've read about, seen in a film or on TV, or that you intend to put in a story. Write as though you were that person.
- Note down what *you* think are your achievements over the past week/month. Are any of these different from what other people say you have achieved?
- Write about what has made you happy recently, or proud, or what has made you laugh. (You're allowed to write down jokes too!)
- Write down the wisest thing you've heard or read recently.
- Notice somebody you've never met and don't know. Based on what you observe, write a diary entry for yesterday/the past week as though you were that person.
- Keep a diary written from the point of view of your pet.
- Keep a diary based on a 'what if' (p. 35). So what if there were two species of humans in the world, one like ourselves and one that could only be outside at night (they are not vampires by the way)? Either be yourself or one of the 'other species' and keep a diary of what has happened recently.
- Consider writing your next story in the form of a diary.

Tip: For those children who do maintain a diary, based on either one of the ideas above or a more conventional record, get them to look back several months. If they wish they can tell you/their friends their reaction.

CHARACTER STEW

This is a light-hearted but useful way of helping children to think about themselves. Ask them to imagine that people are like a 'stew' made of different ingredients. So I might be: a good rich stock of experience, plenty of humour cut into large chunks, a pinch of annoyance at having to queue, a hint of cynicism but no trace of bitterness, lashings of optimism and now and again some down-in-the-dumplings.

Tip: Look at recipe books for appropriate vocabulary that children can include in their descriptions. Key 'culinary vocabulary' or 'words found in recipes' into a search engine for plenty of terms such as – al dente, aromatic, bake, broil, broth, combine, kneed, soupçon, sauté, etc.

Extend the activity by comparing feelings with flavours, textures and aromas, herbs, spices and other ingredients. So anger might be chilli pepper, lemon juice would be sour, sugar would be sweet… What would loyalty be? Or a sense of humour? Or shyness?

GATHERING TREASURES

This is the act of seeking out and noting down ideas, memories, insights and snippets of wisdom that focus on the positive and the inspirational. Gathering treasures can take various forms:

- Give children some quiet time to remember positive things that they or others have done. This might be something as simple as making a friend smile, sharing a bag of crisps, being patient, holding back from making a criticism or negative judgement, paying someone a compliment.

Tip: Asking a child to go on such a 'treasure hunt' can often offset the unhelpful impact of self-limiting beliefs or a negative self-assessment.

- *A treasure box of ideas.* This is literally a box where children can put their positive thoughts, helpful suggestions, inspirational quotes etc. The idea started off as an adjunct to the coin flip game (p. **39**) used for storymaking. Sometimes a child would have a great idea, ask it as a yes-no question and the coin would come up 'no'. Then I would make the point that all ideas have potential and invite that child to jot down his thought on a piece of paper and post it in the treasure box. Periodically as a class we'd look through the box and use some of the ideas as the basis for discussion or for making another story.

- *'Thank You' display.* This is simply a display space where children can publicly thank others for positive things said and done. On one thank you board I noticed some delightful messages, where one child thanked the grey sky for not raining on her as she walked to school, and where a boy thanked his cat for purring when he stroked her.

THE WISE OBSERVER

In the area of emotional resourcefulness there is an idea called the wise observer or 'the one who watches wisely'. If I am angry then it is the wise observer part of me who stands back, as it were, and notices me being angry. He may wonder why the anger is there and whether it needs to be and, if so, is it reasonable, proportionate and *useful* in helping me to learn and grow.

The wise observer in other words does not get caught up in and carried away by negative emotions. He is also the one who reflects on how any emotion could potentially be a positive resource (see the principle of positive purposes on page **110**). He is the one who notices my mental chatter, the assumptions I make, the conclusions I jump to, the knee jerk responses that are sometimes so easily made.

The wise observer may also be the wise adviser, suggesting what I could best think, feel, say and do in a given situation. He is the one who can give practical tips for exploiting the positive energy of aspiration and ambition, saying in effect, 'Yes you'd like to achieve that. How can you go about it? As a first step why don't you try…'

The root of 'wise' is shared by 'wizard' (Middle English *wysard*, a wise man). In helping children to understand the concept of the wise observer we can personify the idea as Wizzy the Wizard (see Figure 5.3).

Figure 5.3 Wizzy the Wizard

Wizzy is that part of our selves who can do all of the things mentioned above. He might also substitute for Merlin in the Merlin Game (p. **25**) and represent the wizard of our imagination with his capacity to create ideas and transform our thoughts and feelings. He is the one who can help us to see the world and ourselves more positively. He can leap into the future and allow us to visualise the kind of life we want to make for ourselves. He can offer understanding and friendship to our 'younger selves' when upsetting memories appear. He can also recognise the kind, helpful, noble things we've done and remind us of those events, thus helping to raise our self-esteem which, truly speaking, is the way we estimate ourselves.

WISDOM TALES

Parables and fairy tales are a great source of wise advice, albeit sometimes couched in metaphor and symbolism. As such they operate partly at a subconscious level: the child will assimilate the teachings in the story, associating them with her own experiences. The result of such 'behind the scenes' processing is the heightened probability of insights and creative solutions popping into mind 'out of the blue'. Eureka moments often happen in this way rather than being the result of methodical conscious reasoning.

Stories often allow children to understand – again tacitly – the elements and structure of a narrative. Of course children realise that a story usually has a hero, a villain, a problem that needs to be solved and a quest involving challenges to achieve this. But stories also communicate heroic qualities such as determination in the face of setbacks, humility, selflessness, being wary of overconfidence, and others. The hero's quest will necessarily have its obstacles and challenges, the 'learning ground' that allows the hero to realise those qualities. Another important feature of many such tales is the fact that the hero is human; he or she can be vulnerable, flawed and in need of help. As such 'heroism' in this light is something that is potentially available to all of us.

Children's own stories can serve the purpose of expressing and working through a problem, sometimes without the child herself realising this at first. The resolution of the story might contain the seeds of a solution to the real life issue. Aside from this, simply getting the matter off your chest by writing it out creates a fresh perspective from which to view it.

There are many excellent collections of wisdom tales. Many of the stories are very short and would take only a few minutes to read or tell. Books I recommend include:

- *Zen Flesh, Zen Bones* by Paul Reps (1980)
- *The Commanding Self* by Idries Shah (1997)
- *Stories for the Third Ear* by Lee Wallas (1985)
- *How Stories Heal* by Pat Williams (2009).

There are also books available on the power of metaphor in stories such as David Hodgson's (2010) *Magic of Modern Metaphor* and Nick Owen's (2002) *The Magic of Metaphor*.

READY, AIM, GO

Solving problems in any area is as much a matter of the *will* to solve them as being armed with the necessary 'how to' techniques. Method must be matched with motivation. The techniques themselves, by giving children a pathway to achievement, tend to increase children's willingness to apply themselves, while we can 'model the behaviour' through our own enthusiasm and our confidence in their effectiveness.

Another useful technique is the 'coaching buddy', where the teacher or classmate helps to give focus and direction to a child seeking a solution to a problem. The necessary steps are to ask these questions in this order:

What do you want?
Although this question sounds obvious, clearly defining the problem at the outset can save much time and effort later on. The

answer should be in the affirmative. So rather than saying, 'I don't want to get poor marks in literacy' the child should reframe this to, 'I want to get better marks in literacy.'

How will you get there?

This invites the child to plan a route towards the solution in some detail. Although the coaching buddy might have ideas, he should not simply jump in with his own thoughts – 'Well I think you should do this...' is contrary to the principle of independent thinking.

The 'coachee' might say she doesn't know how to solve the problem, in which case the coaching buddy with a light touch needs to prompt and guide with a question like, 'How do you think x would tackle this?' or, 'If you did know, what would you do?' This sounds absurd at first though makes more sense when we remember that we know more than we think we do. It also creates the opportunity for the coachee to realise her own creativity and flexibility as a problem solver.

The aim of this stage of the process is not just to formulate a general plan of action but also to break it down into smaller more easily doable chunks. So if the coachee decides to get better marks in literacy by 'working harder' the coach could step in here by asking, 'What does that mean exactly?' or, 'How will you achieve that aim?'

Questioning and prompting in this way will ideally allow the coachee to create a detailed and achievable strategy for solving the problem. The next step is to begin – to take direct positive action – which the coaching buddy can help to facilitate by questions such as, 'So what will you do first?' and, 'When will you have done that?' Building reasonable deadlines into the plan heightens the chances of it succeeding.

How did it go?

This question prompts a review and assessment, either of each step towards a solution or of the whole strategy once it has been applied. The coaching buddy can aid this process by asking what went particularly well, what didn't go so well (and why), what else could be done and what has been learned during the process of finding a solution.

We have only just touched on the notion of buddy coaching as an adjunct to children's thinking and problem solving skills. To find out more see *Coaching Emotional Intelligence in the Classroom* (Bowkett & Percival, 2011).

HERE AND NOW

Eckhart Tolle's (2005) book *The Power of Now* uses the powerful symbol of the hourglass to help us realise that whatever has happened in the past and whatever the future might bring, we only exist in this present instant. We only have direct influence over the single sand grain passing through the waist of the hourglass right now. While we can draw upon our resources of memory and imagination to learn from our experiences and plan ahead, there is great value in appreciating the amazing fact of our own existence at this moment.

The spontaneous energy, enthusiasm and playfulness in so many children are in a way a living demonstration of this. Just as children are naturally curious and creative, so by and large do they value the here and now. As adults we can learn from them, even as we can teach them a bundle of techniques for solving problems before or as they arise so that their appreciation of the world and enjoyment of life can be enhanced.

Regardless of what other techniques and strategies you offer the children, occasionally take a minute to let them 'be here now'.

Bibliography

Asimov, I. (1974) *Words of Science*. London: George Harrap & Co. Ltd.

Bowkett, S. (1999) *Self-Intelligence*. Stafford: Network Educational Press.

Bowkett, S. (2007) *Jumpstart! Creativity*. Abingdon, Oxon.

Bowkett, S. (2010) *Developing Literacy and Creative Writing Through Storymaking: Story Strands for 7–12-Year-Olds*. Maidenhead: Open University Press.

Bowkett, S. & Percival, S. (2011) *Coaching Emotional Intelligence in the Classroom*. Hove: Routledge.

Buckley, J. (2011) *Pocket P4C: Getting Started with Philosophy for Children*. Chelmsford, Essex: One Slice Books.

Carnagie, D. (1972) *How to Stop Worrying and Start Living*. Tadworth, Surrey: World's Work.

Claxton, G. & Lucas, B. (2004) *Be Creative*. London: BBC Books.

Dweck, C. (2000) *Self-Theories: Their Role in Motivation, Personality and Development*. New York: Psychology Press.

Egan, K. (1986) *Teaching As Story Telling*. Ontario: University of Chicago Press.

Hodgson, D. (2010) *Magic of Modern Metaphor*. Bancyfelin, Carmarthen: Crown House.

Law, S. (2000) *The Philosophy Files*. London: Orion.

Law, S. (2003) *The Philosophy Files 2*. London: Orion.

Owen, N. (2002) *The Magic of Metaphor*. Bancyfelin, Carmarthen: Crown House.

Perkins, D. (2000) *The Eureka Effect*. New York: Norton.

Reps, P. (1980) *Zen Flesh, Zen Bones*. Harmondsworth, Middlesex: Penguin Books.

Rockett, M. & Percival, S. (2002) *Thinking for Learning*. Stafford, Network Educational Press.

Shah, I. (1997) *The Commanding Self*. London: Octagon Press.

Stanley, S. & Bowkett, S. (2004) *But Why? Developing Philosophical Thinking in the Classroom*. Stafford: Network Educational Press.

Stock, G. (2004) *The Kids' Book of Questions*. New York: Workman.

Tolle, E. (2005) *The Power of Now*. London: Hodder and Stoughton.

Von Oech, R. (1990) *A Whack on the Side of the Head: How You Can Be More Creative*. London: HarperCollins.

Wallas, L. (1985) *Stories for the Third Ear*. New York: Norton.

Whitehead, A. N. (1961) *Adventures of Ideas*. Cambridge: Cambridge University Press.

Williams, P. (2009) *How Stories Heal* [audiobook]. London: Human Givens Publishing.

Solution to the puzzle on page **71:** Janet and John are goldfish.